Basics of Hinduism

Questions Concerning

Sanatan Dharma

Author

Kamlakant Tripathi

Preface

Hinduism or Sanatan Dharma means the eternal religion, the ancient Law. It is based on the Vedas. This religion has also been called the Aryan Religion because it is the religion that was given to the first nation of the Aryan race. But alas! Some of us donot know its different aspects correctly. Also, there are some demerits, defects and flaws in this religion which we should also know and shun their practices.

Keeping this in view, the book has been written mentioning its different positive-negative aspects. It contains its all plus as well as minus points. All pros and cons of the subject are honestly elaborated. The author does not like appeasement. The book may be quarrelsome or nagging for some people, but learning like this is a must. The author, Shri Kamlakant Tripathi, is a former Professor at Gorakhpur University and retired Chief Commissioner at Revenue Department, Government of India.

Its motto is to spread the learning of Hinduism in correct sense withour boasting anyhow. Readers are requested to go through the book thoroughly. You will find bits of knowledge and points of learning. You may also find some defects and demerits of this religion which you should shun practising summarily.

While publishing this book, we took utmost care to make it error free. However, to err is human. Errors crept in inadvertently, if any, may please be brought to our notice. Comments and suggestions are most welcome.

-Ram Nivas Kumar

Contents

Part-I

1

Is Hinduism a 'Religion'?

Is Hinduism a 'religion' in accepted sense of the term as used in the English language? No. a Hindu can very well call himself areligious. Even being a 'believer' is not sine qua non for being a Hindu. In fact, there being no concept of ex-communication or blasphemy in Hinduism, a person born a Hindu remains a Hindu unless he himself discards his Hindu identity. There is no recognized institution or authority to declare such a person to have become a non-Hindu.

In Sanskrit, the word dharma (धर्म) as a noun is etymologically derived from the root dhri (धृ) to mean that which ordains and sustains the universe—ध्रियतेलोकोऽनेन इति धर्म:. At micro level, it becomes the real nature of things. Here 'real' is quite close to Aristotelian or teleological concept of nature, where nature of a thing is the 'idea' of that thing as distinct from its imperfect expressions conditioned by umpteen factors subject to time and space, taking its color from the ultimate end that it strives to reach. Roughly speaking, the dharma of salt is to be salty and that of sugar to be sweet and, likewise, of man to be human. It is only then that the universe is sustained giving meaning to Dharma at macro level.

In ancient texts, the word 'rit (ऋत) and satya (सत्य) are synonymous with dharma. In fact, the word dharma came in use later when rit and satya were already in vogue. Rit connotes immutable, incorporeal law that holds the universe, quite akin to Ancient Greek tradition of Natural Law as propounded by Heraclitus. Satya (truth) is of much wider connotation but it also remains immutable by definition. Rit Sukta (ऋत सूक्त) of Rigveda (10-190) uses the two words as complementary to each other—ऋतं च सत्यं चाभीद्धात्तपसोऽध्यजायत। ततोरात्र्यजायत तत: समुद्रो अर्णव:॥ [It is from the penance that first rit and satya were born, then night (darkness) was born, then was born the undulating ocean.] Later, dharma came to replace both rit and satya. So, dharma is primordial truth that constitutes basic nature of things as also that sustains the universe in its course. By its nature, dharma has to be without beginning and end (sanatan). Neither the basic attributes of a thing nor that which sustains the universe comprises such things as go on changing.

True, in that sense, the translation of 'secular' cannot be 'dharma-nirapeksha' (धर्म-निरपेक्ष). In fact, nothing in the universe can be dharma-nirapeksha. But since, in the course of time, dharma has come to be used as synonymous with the system of beliefs and practices, it is futile to enter into a debate as to the appropriateness or otherwise of the term 'dharma-nirapeksha' as translation of 'secular'. Granted the word secular carries a peculiar concept historically evolved in an altogether different milieu--it was first used in the sense of temporal to limit the sphere of ecclesiastical or spiritual authority in Europe of Middle Ages and not to alienate the state from different religious groups inhabiting its territory. The dispute then was between the authority of the Church and that of the State and not between the treatment to be meted out to different religions in the same state so as to bring the relevance of the state's insulation or otherwise from them. It is only later that it came to assume the meaning that currently prevails. But what is there in the name! Nobody will dispute the fact that no state, rather no institution can be divorced from the basic truth of existence even if it strives to. Whether one uses the word pantha-nirpeksha (पंथ निरपेक्ष) or dharma-nirpeksha, both are currently understood to convey the same meaning as secular. But the problem arises when one doesn't object to dharma being used in the sense of religion-- the system of beliefs and practices-- but objects to the use of dharma-nirpeksha as the translation of secular.

The question whether Hinduism as it is practiced to-day imbibes dharma equivalent to rit and satya? It would be too naive or too fanatical to say so. The question boils down to what precisely constitutes dharma as equivalent to rit and satya that sustains the universe and, at the same time, constitutes the real nature of things comprising the universe.

In fact, the Hindu concept of dharma (as equivalent to rit and satya) is too generic to serve any tangible purpose in day-to-day practical life. No one being repository of rit and satya, everybody has to explore what is dharma for him. This is what is meant by Sanskrit word adhyatm (अध्यात्म) that is generally used as equivalent to spirituality of English. Adhyatm, adhi+atm (अधि+आत्म) means that which concerns self. There is no scope of intermediary or external help in adhyatm. One can write, discuss, explain, guide but cannot dictate. Following of such dictates remains blind faith or superstition for the subject unless he gets convinced by virtue of his own level of understanding and the faculty of reasoning. Even if it may not be a blind faith for the person trying to convince by virtue of his more developed faculties or some 'higher' (?) experience. In fact, faith, in order to be true faith, must be blind; if it is not blind, it may be anything but not 'faith'. Thus, there is hardly any difference between faith and blind faith. In Hindu tradition, most of the texts containing discourse on 'dharma', which are nothing but philosophical discourses, are in dialogue form. Most of the Upanishads as also their compendium Gita are in this form basically meant for the curious who puts question after question before getting convinced. Reading or listening of these discourses by others may not help except for providing diversionary relief of temporary nature akin to 'shmashan vairagya' (श्मशान वैराग्य)-- renunciation induced by cremation ground. Ever-increasing number of Babas of different hues currently doing brisk business of preaching before huge crowds is at best aberrations. The concluding part of almost all Hindu philosophical texts and the epics and the Puranas (even Tulsidas's Ramacharitmanas in Awadhi dialect of Hindi) contains an injunction against indiscriminate communication, laying down that these are not to be imparted to anyone who doesn't deserve. But who bothers when power and pelf are involved, a credulous audience is available in abundance seeking diversion and even atonement of day-to-day unprincipled wrongdoings inescapably causing some chasm of conscience.

It is true; these concepts of dharma and adhyatm render dharma as extremely elusive. It is this elusiveness or the lack of categorical assertion about many concrete principles that, to my understanding, is the essence of Hunduism. This should normally make Hinduism extremely catholic, eclectic, flexible, accommodating and tolerant so as to encompass the whole humanity, rather whole creation. Is it so in practice? It is apparent that on account of free and spontaneous development spanning millennia, this essence has been shrouded by layer after layer of deviations as well as embellishments, some sublime, some perfunctory and even harmful.

Nevertheless, it is this elusiveness that accounts for the co-existence of innumerable sects within the Hindu fold, encompassing infinite number of gods and goddesses and innumerable practices of worship and belief systems without being viewed as deviation from the basic concept of Hinduism. Both monism (अद्वैतवाद) of Shankaracharya and dualism (द्वैतवाद) of Madhvacharya, with finer variations of vishishtadvait (विशिष्टाद्वैत) of Ramanujacharya, dvaitadvait (द्वैताद्वैत) of Nimbarkacharya, shuddhadvait (शुद्धाद्वैत) of Vallabhacharya and achintyabhedabhed (अचिन्त्यभेदाभेद) of Chaitanya and his Goswamipads, can flourish without any marked conflict. These are in fact schools of philosophy propounded by different acharyas coming in succession after Shankar (788 AD to 820 AD), the only commonality being that all of them claim solidarity with Vedas. And these are the variations in only one school, i.e. Vedanta, out of six schools of Hindu philosophy that claim adherence to Vedas. Non-Vedic schools of Lokayata, Jain and Buddhist, although imbibing more or less the same Indian spirit, stand apart. It is again on account of lack of definite assertion on many aspects that several strands of rituals and practices in Hinduism purport to follow schools of philosophy involving more or less free thinking and not any revealed truth.

2

Is Hinduism Based on 'Revealed' Knowledge?

Vedas are called Shruti (श्रुति) and Apourusheya (अपौरुषेय) or Aptawakya (आप्तवाक्य). Shruti carries two meanings— (1) that which is not composed by human beings but heard from an incorporeal source, the divine voice, and (2) that which is transmitted through generations by means of hearing and memorizing. Apourusheya is again that which is not created by human efforts. And Aptawakya is that which is axiomatic or divine truth and cannot be questioned by logic. There seems to be nothing in Vedas themselves to support the former meaning of Shruti at the exclusion of the latter. There is also nothing therein that supports the concept of Apaurusheya and Aptawakya. These words do not occur in four Samhitas—Rigved, Saamved, Yajurved and Atharvaved nor in Brahmanas, Aranyakas, and Upanishadas which are included in the expansive meaning of Shrutis. It appears, later commentators added these epithets out of reverence. Thus, Hinduism is not based on any revelation and, to the western mind, that being one of the necessary attributes of religion, it is not a religion in accepted sense of the term, That is another reason why there is unlimited freedom to choose one's own path. One may go for devotion to his chosen aradhya (आराध्य) or isht (इष्ट) god with or without idol worship (सगुणोपासना)--idol being symbolic representation of some selected attributes of that infinite being (Bhakti cult—भक्तिमार्ग). Or, one may revel in the experience of that ultimate, incorporeal, cosmic reality referred to as निराकार ब्रह्म through knowledge (Jnyan cult--ज्ञान मार्ग). One need not even have belief either in a personified God or in any cogitative, ultimate cosmic reality, he may be content with the perception of creation as the combination of consciousness and physical world (पुरुष and प्रकृति), which are not amenable to propitiation by any means available to humans, thus leaving him to fend for himself in managing his affairs as per his own understanding of the nature of self and the surrounding world. One may derive purposefulness and fulfilment by doing the duty of his station with best of his ability and also spiritual equipoise by seeking excellence in whatever he is assigned to do with such involvement as to render the gains and results as redundant (Karma cult—कर्म मार्ग).

It logically follows that it is not open to Bhakti-margi or Jnyan margi to question anything that he may perceive as unjust and unpalatable in the world around him, because he has to have a firm belief in the divine hand behind whatever happens or doesn't happen and unconditionally surrender before the God's play, leaving no scope for dissatisfaction on any account whatsoever. It is left only to a Karma-margi to try to contribute his bit in setting things right as per his own understanding of the existence, with due sensitivity towards others and without bothering about the results of his honest and dedicated efforts (निष्काम कर्मयोग of गीता). When the so-called great devotees, or those claiming to have understood the riddles of existence with reference to Godly presence, air dissatisfaction over worldly affairs, a doubt irresistibly arises as to the genuineness of their faith in the

Godly presence. This contradiction is common to almost all religions that believe in inviolable divine will and, at the same time, prompt their followers to take up the task of setting things right even at the cost of killing human beings, the most beautiful creation {ashraful makhluq (अश्रफुल मख़्लूक़)} of the God Almighty.

One core issue of confusion. The Hindus' catholic and generic approach doesn't work when Hinduism encounters a proselytizing religion based on exclusive, unitary concept of truth as revealed by one personified God through one prophet in one book incorporating all relevant details and specifics. Even though a Hindu may regard such religion as yet another way of realizing the basic, primordial truth of existence, to a genuine follower of that revealed religion, he will be a pretender, a pagan and an infidel on account of not conforming to the premises with details and specifics laid down in his book of revealed truth. So, the catholicity helps only when matched with corresponding catholicity. Many Hindus either evade this predicament or refuse to realize its implication and tend to adopt self-righteous posture of a much-wronged people.

3

Unhindered Quest of the Unknown

Another basic element of Hinduism is constant quest of the unknown. Absence of the claim of revealed knowledge gave child-like curiosity combined with extraordinary intuitive grasp of the phenomenon of creation in an effort to place the man in this mysterious phalanx of existence. Upanishads contain some of the most illuminating contemplative efforts free from the bondage of any presumption or dogma to grasp the ultimate reality. The roots are there in the most ancient religious text of Rigveda declaring Ekam sad vipra bahudha vadanti (एकं सद् विप्रा बहुधा वदंति), Roughly translated, it means, He is one but Brahmavettas (those having knowledge of Brahman, the ultimate reality) describe him in many ways.

Here, one is tempted to quote the famous seven verses of one of the oldest pieces of Rigveda— Nasadiya Sukta (नासदीय सूक्त)—10.129.1-7:--

नासदासीन्त्रो सदासीत्तदानीं नासीद्रजो नो व्योमा परो यत्।
किमावरीय: कुह कस्य शर्मन्नम्भ: किमासीद् गहनं
गभीरम्॥1॥

[Then there was no non-existent nor existent; there was no realm of air, no sky beyond it. What covered in, and where? And what gave shelter? Was water there, unfathomed depth of water?]

न मृत्युरासीदमृतं न तर्हि न रात्र्या अह्न आसीत् प्रकेत:।
अनीदवातं स्वधया तदेकं तस्माद्धान्यन्न पर: किं
चनास॥2॥

[Death was not there, nor was there anything immortal; no sign was there, the day's and night's divider. That one thing, breathless, breathed by its own nature; apart from it there was nothing whatsoever]

तमआसीत्तमसा गूहमग्रेsप्रकेतं सलिलं सर्वमा इदम्
।तुच्छ्येनाभ्वपिहितं यदासीत् तपसस्तन्महिनाजायतैकम् ॥3॥

[Darkness there was, at first concealed in darkness, this all was indiscriminate chaos. All that existed then was void and formless; by the

great power of warmth was born that
unit.]

कामस्तदग्रे समवर्तताधि मनसो रेत: प्रथमं यदासीत्। सतो
बंधुमसति निरविन्दन् हृदि प्रतीष्या कवयो मनीषा॥4॥

[Thereafter rose desire in the
beginning, desire the primal seed and
germ of spirit. Sages who searched
with their heart's thought discovered
the existent's kinship in the non-
existent.]

तिरश्चीनो विततो रश्मिरेषा मध: स्विदासीदुपरि स्विदासीत्।
रेतोधा आसन् महिमान आसन् स्वधा अवस्तात् प्रयति:
परस्तात्॥5॥

[Transversely was their severing line
extended? What was above it then, and
what below it? There were begetters,
there were mighty forces, free action
here and energy over there.]

को अद्धा वेद क इह प्र वोचत् कुत आजाता कुत इयं
विसृष्टि:। अर्वाग् देवा अस्य विसर्जनेनाऽथा को वेद यत
आवभूव॥6॥

[Who verily knows and who can here
declare it, whence it was born and
whence comes this creation? The gods
are later than this word's production.

Who knows then whence it first came into being?]

इयंविसृष्टिर्यत आबभूव यदि वा दधे यदि वा न। यो अस्याध्यक्ष: परमे व्योमन् त्सो अङ्ग वेद यदि वा न वेद॥7॥

[He, the first origin of this creation, whether he formed it all or did not form it. Whose eye controls this world in highest heaven, he verily knows it, or perhaps he knows it not.]

{English translation from 'Hindu Scriptures' as quoted in 'The Discovery of India', p.58, second ed., 1946.}

With my limited exposure, I have not come across such approximation to current cosmological discourse on creation in any other scripture. Science is still grappling with the questions that were raised and left unanswered in Nasadiya Sukta. Big Bang of Stephan Hawking has since been seriously questioned by many scientists. And what is striking about this Sukta is it is the result of not any scientific analysis but only honest contemplation with a potent intuitive power without any presumptuous reference to the God's role, though, ironically, Max Muller gave it the title :'To the Unknown God'. It is only befitting that Shyam Benegal has used lyrical Hindi translation of these verses as the title song of his world-class serial, Bharat Ek Khoj, based on Nehru's Discovery of India.

This is quite in contrast with the gross formulations about creation in Purush Sukta (पुरुष सूक्त) of the same, 10th Mandal of Rigveda. This Purush Sukta contains that infamous but oft-quoted verse prescribing the order of four Varnas (to me, it appears to be later interpolation)—ब्राह्मणोऽस्य मुखमासीद् बाहू राजन्य: कृत:। ऊरू तदस्य यद्वैश्य: पद्भ्यां शूद्रोऽजायत. [The Brahmins were his mouth, the Kshatriyas were created as his arms, Vaishyas were his thighs and Shudras were born of his feet.]

This brings us to the origin and development of Varna or Caste systems in Hinduism.

Part-II

Varna and Caste Systems

No society in the world has ever been free from inhuman devices of exploitation of man by man by enslavement and subjugation of those who happened to be weak under the force of circumstances. Slavery associated with the cruel practice of forcing free people to become slaves on victory over them and revolting process of trade and export of slaves had been an accepted way of life in all ancient civilizations including Egyptian, Greek and Roman—Roman legions turned most of their captives and even the inhabitants of conquered territories into slaves at will. The evil continued through the middle ages to the earlier centuries of the modern age. Even before it was slowly abolished, serfs had replaced slaves who later turned into proletariat after industrial revolution. The condition of proletariat (having no possession but for the body which they were forced to hire out at minimum sustenance wages) was of course pathetic but it was far better than those of the serfs who were not free to change their masters and were frequently whipped. That is why, after industrial revolution, the serfs fled from rural estates to turn proletariat in cities in such large numbers as to leave many constituencies (termed as pocket burrows and rotten burrows in England) leaving few voters who could easily be purchased by political aspirants. The condition of slaves, in turn, was much worse than their successor serfs. But great pace of industrialization slowly did away with the traditional distinction between commoners and gentlemen though economic differences and class distinctions still persist. In India, the story of castes and varnas, though served the same purpose of exploitation, is quite unique. Its nature is materially different and its development presents one of the most complex and controversial aspects of this old and continuing civilization.

Varna or caste systems which are intertwined are, however, not basic to Hinduism. It is difficult to find a convincing answer as to the origin of this cancerous growth in the Hindu society and how the fifth Varna (पंचम वर्ण) of Dalits (earlier Antyajas, Untouchables or Scheduled Castes) came into being. Except in one verse of Purush Sukta which elaborately deals with the creation of different elements and constituents of the universe including four Varnas in the society, there appears to be no reference in Rigveda of Varnas or Castes, their respective rights and duties and privileges and disadvantages e.t.c. The aforesaid verse--ब्राह्मणोऽस्य मुखमासीद् बाहू राजन्य: कृत:। ऊरू तदस्य यद्वैश्य: पद्भ्यां शूद्रोऽजायत (10.90.12) [The Brahmins were his mouth, the Kshatriyas were created as his arms, Vaishyas were his thighs and Shudras were born of his feet.] stands alone. The picture that emerges from otherverses of Rigveda rather goes contrary to the import of this verse. The verses 1.80.16; 1.114.2; 2.33.13; 3.3.6; 4.14.2; 4.37.1; 6.14.2 and 8.52.1 of Rigveda regard Manu as the sole progenitor of people which version was so deep-rooted as to be carried forward to the Brahmans, Puranas, Smritis and Dhramasutras. In one of the verses of Rigveda the poet gives a very significant clue—कारुरहं ततो भिषक् उपलपृक्षिणी नना (1.119.3).[I am a carpenter, my father is a medicine-man and my mother makes dung-cakes). This seems to be a pointer to the fact that during Rigvedic period there were only occupations which had not yet stratified on the basis of birth and heredity. The contradiction is obvious. After being born from four different body parts of that enigmatic Virat Purush (Yajna Purush), how did the progeny of these four got assimilated among themselves to become equal by birth traceable to Manu although following different occupations in the Rigvedic period itself.

In any case, there is no evidence of there being hierarchical organisation of Rigvedic society divided vertically into Varnas and Castes as is found in later periods.

As Colebrooke opines, Purush Sukta is very different in language, metre and stylefrom the rest of the verses of Rigveda dealing with the subject of creation, most eclectic and scientific among them being seven verses of Naasadiya Sukta quoted in the previous part. Purush Sukta must have been composed after the Sanskrit language had been refined and its grammar and rhythm had been perfected. As Prof. Max Muller puts it, the hymn of this

Sukta is of much later origin both in its character and diction. For instance, it mentions the three seasons in the order of Vasanta (Spring), Grishma (Summer) and Sharad (Autumn) whereas the word Grishma does not occur in any other hymn of Rigveda and Vasant is not at all traceable in earlier Vedic vocabulary.

The text of this Sukta also occurs in Yajurveda, Samaveda and Atharvaveda but the same is not uniform nor in the same order.As against 16 verses in Rigveda and Atharvaveda,there are 22 in Yajurveda and only 5 in Samaveda. The liberty that the authors of different Samhitas took in recording these verses indicates that they did not regard this Sukta to be an ancient composition. In Rigveda this Sukta occurs in miscellaneous segment and in Atharvaveda in supplementary segment which clearly points that it was composed and interpolated at a later stage. This Sukta is not found in Maitrayani, Taittiriya and Kathaka Samhitas of Krishna Yajurveda which is a clear pointer to the fact that it was not therein Rigveda at least before these Samhitas were composed. The entire evidence goes to prove the views of Max Muller and others that Purush Sukta was a later interpolation and Varna System is neither Rigvedic nor divine.

Many current theoriesabout the origin of this monstrous hierarchy in Hindu society, particularly those propounded by the leftist historians do not stand the test of fact andreason; some of them also appear motivated. Particularly the racial theory advancing the view that Aryans came from outside and subdued original (Dravidian?) settlors whom they referred to as Asuras or Dasyus or Rakshasas and later assimilated them in their fold as Shudras. And Dalitswere those of the Shudras who fought more valiantly and were crushed andreduced to a more degradedposition rendering them untouchables.

Rigveda does mention two major groups of gods: Devas and Asuras, but unlike in later texts, Asuras are not demonized there. Aditi is the mother of Agni (of Deva group) as well as Asuras (Adityas) to which group two prominent gods Mitra and Varun belong. If thetheory of Aryan invasion and racial struggle is accepted, animosity should have been more pronounced in the earlier stages of clash than in the later stages of assimilation.

I found a queer phenomenon in the leftist intellectuals. They regard the acceptance of racial theory of Aryan migration and domination of aboriginals as the proof of being Marxist and the acceptance of their indigenous origin as the proof of being cultural nationalist (Dhananjay Verma, Lahak, April-September 2019). The issue is not Marxist but purely academic and has to be determined by honest and sincere research and objective analysis of the material gathered and that already available.

From the very beginning of the historical period, the Aryans and the so-called non-Aryans have been found living together in India. The natural presumption would be that they belong here. If a proposition is made that Aryans came from outside and established their domain over the aboriginals by force and then assimilated them in their own fold as Sudras and untouchables, the onus of adducing reasonable evidence lies on the one who claims this. If this proposition is prima facie proved, it is then only that the onus will shift to the person who claims Aryans to be indigenous. So far, this proposition has not been proved except by twisting and imagining facts first by the colonial historians as a matter of their imperial design to divide the society and then by the Marxist historians to advance the cause of their ideology, resorting to politics of conflict and degrading the cultural past of India by all available means.

What are the components of the proof required? First, that the 'Aryans' constitute a race different from that of the aboriginals. Then, for the Aryans being themigrants of pre-historic period, it has to be determined conclusively wherefrom they came to India. Then the reason and time of their migration from the said region has to be ascertained with reasonable degree of certainty on the basis of authentic material.Then comes the proof of migration by way of invasion, victory over aboriginals and their assimilation while keeping the contempt and racial prejudice alive for millennia.

A race may be defined as a body of people possessing certain common physical traits which are hereditary. According to Max Muller the word Aryan is used in Sanskrit in four different senses. The owner of ploughed land (अर्य); one who ploughs or tills; body of people; (Panini's

Ashtadhyayi,1.103); and of noble origin. There occur two words in Rigveda—अर्य (Arya) and आर्य (Aarya), the word अर्य is used at 88 places with four distinct meanings, namely, enemy, respectable person, India, and owner or citizen (Vaishya). The word आर्य is used at 33 places but nowhere in the sense of race. Max Muller, once staunch proponent of Aryan race theory, later became wiser after adequate studies. He then held:

"There is no Aryan race in blood; Aryan in scientific language is utterly inapplicable to race. It means language and nothing but language; and if we speak of Aryan race at all, we should know that it means no more than Aryan speech" (Science of Language).

And where did the Aryans come from? There is a bewildering variety of views:

1.Benfey (as summarized by Prof. Isaac Tayler)—Eastward of Caspian Sea and North of the Black Sea.

2.Geiger—North-West of Black Sea.

3.Prof. Ripley—Caucasia

4.Lokmanya Tilak—Arctic Region

5.Jyotiba Phule (Ghulamgiri)—Iran or Persia

And the answer topertinent question when and why the Aryans migrated to India is not even attempted by the theorists of invasionand domination. It still remains unanswered.

As regards the purpose of migration being invasion and subjugation of the aboriginals, there is not even an iota of evidence suggesting the invasion of India by the people of Aryan race from outside and subjugation of her native tribes. P T Srinivasa Iyengar refutes any such suggestion on the basis of the occurrence of the words Arya, Dasa and Dasyu where these terms refer to cult and not race. The testimony of the Vedic literature is rather against the theory that the original home of Aryans was outside India. The endearing and emotional language in which the seven rivers of India are addressed by Aryans--my Ganges, my Yamuna and my Saraswati (Rigveda 10.75.5), no foreigner would ever do. In the vast literature of Vedic and Laukik Sanskrit beginning with Rigveda not even a shred of memory of any earlier homeland of Aryans is traceable. This required a grand conspiracy to be perpetuated from generation to generation to obliterate the memory of homeland which is impossible in the face of human nature as it is. The indentured labor (Girmitia or Jahajis) shipped by the British from India to Fiji, Mauritius, South Africa, Trinidad and Tobago, Guyana, Surinam Jamaica etc. for sugarcane plantation during nineteenth and early twentieth century still carry the memory of their local Indian foods, dress, language, folklores religious texts (they carried copies of Ramcharitmanas with them) and family tree; theystill constitute a strong Indian diaspora settled in different parts of the world.Babur, the first Moghul Emperor, who came from Farghana in Central Asia, writes his Baburnama in Chagatai and fondly remembers history, geography, people, plants and animals of the areas he lived, the battles and weapons he fought with and the family chronicles, music, poetry, wines and historical monuments of that area. The British Americans earned their Independence after an unequal, bloody war with the British but kept the memory of their homeland intact. They named more than a dozen cities after the cities of England by adding the epithet 'New".

The whole area where they first settled on the western coast in America is called 'New England'. People of this area still keep the old British accent and other habits which is ridiculed by calling them Boston Brahmins.

The fact is that in prehistoric period itself, in the course of famous intercontinental movement, several people and races came to settle on the fertile land of different parts of Indian Sub-continent and got intermingled by blood and habits in the course of time. Most common use of Arya and Aryaa (feminine) in Sanskrit is to show respect to an elder and accomplished. The wife addresses her husband as Aryaputra and the sons, younger brothers and disciples address their fathers, elder brothers and Gurus respectively as Arya, that doesn't denote that the formers are Anaryas or aboriginals.

This is what Dr. Ambedkar has to say on the futility of this racial theory—

"As a matter of fact Caste system came into being long after the different races of India had co-mingled in blood and culture. To hold that distinctions of Caste are really distinctions of race and treat different Castes as though they were so many different races is a gross perversion of facts. What racial affinity is there between the Brahmin of the Punjab and the Brahmin of Madras? What racial affinity is there between the untouchable of Bengal and the untouchable of Madras? What racial difference is there between the Brahmin of the Punjab and the Chamar of the Punjab? What racial difference is there between the Brahmin of Madras and the pariah of Madras? The Brahmin of the Punjab is racially of the same stock as the Chamar of the Punjab and the Brahmin of Madras is of the same race as the Pariah of Madras. Caste system does not demarcate racial division. Caste system is a social division of the people of the same race." [Writings and Speeches Vol. 1 (2-Annihilation of Caste), p.48, Education Deptt, Government of Maharashtra, 1989]

The development of castes and Varnas in Hindu society is a long-drawn process stretched over a millennia. As shown above, in Rigvedic period there were only occupations or vocationsas mark of identity of a person and there was no hierarchy therein, the father, mother and the son following different vocations without any ignominy attached to any. Gradually these occupations and professions turned hereditary which provided certainty, security of employment and occasion to realize meaning of life through excellence in their assigned work. This also ensured skill and expertise in the profession followed from generation to generation. It is ironical that the society as a whole reaped immense benefits from this skill and expertise for a long time. The production of handicrafts in India was in surplus in quantity and the best in quality in the world. Major market share of world exportbelonged to India being producer of such agricultural goods as were not possible to produce in the climate of Europe and other parts of the then inhabited world except for China and some other eastern countries. Added to this, India produced handicrafts of the best quality in the world. It exported finest muslin, raw silk, spices saltpeter, indigo, iron equipment, edible oils, ghee, Gud and sugar, opium, pearl and precious stones by land routes of silk and spices to Europe via Constantinople as also by sea routes passing through Arabian and Red seas carried on by Arab seafarers. A self-sufficient

India needed very little import and what came in return were only gold and silver bars. The export of spices grown in East-Indies to Europe passed through India and it was also in the hands of Indian sea-traders. This resulted accumulation of immense wealth as well aspeace and prosperity among all classes of people as described in the accounts of Chinese travelers Fa-Hien (405-441 AD), Huen-Tsang (630-648 AD) and I-Tsing (671-695 AD) and the travelers of other countries. It is this wealth and prosperity that entice foreign invaders like Shakas, Kushanas, Huna, Gurjaras and Pratiharas etc who were later got assimilated in caste hierarchy giving rise to Rahput variant of old Kshatriyas. In the end came Turks and Afghans, first as plunderers and then as invaders to settle down and establish their more or less oppressive rule.

It is after the land routes to Constantinople were closed by the Ottoman Turks on their victory over this Byzantinecapitalin 1453 that there was great scramble for search of sea route to India among European powers, use of Indian goods being indispensable for them. Vasco-De-Gama reached India in 1498 and the world changed with the coming of exploitative sea trade of East India Company. It is paradoxical that while country suffered from unstable political conditions in 18th century, its economic prosperity remained phenomenal till that century. It is only after successive colonization of different parts of the country that skilled craftsmen were forced to turn into landless agricultural labour and the burden on agriculture increased tremendously resulting in overall impoverishment of the population which accentuated caste discrimination due to drastic reduction of opportunities.

The darkest chapter of ancient Indian history was turning of horizontal structure of castes into hierarchical structure and birth of untouchability. Scant research has been done on this development and on the factors responsible for its gaining strength after strength so as to become invincible. The process must have taken long years, rather centuries. The sole reason for development of horrific institution of untouchability appears to be obsessive emphasis on purity (शुचिता) which rendered people engaged in certain professions considered unclean as untouchables. As regards hierarchical structure, it must have grown by slow but natural process of gradation of professions and gained strength by psychological yearning of security with an illusory feeling of superiority. It is noteworthy that each caste had superior as well inferior castes to look at. Whereas the firstone gave a feeling of inferiority, the second gave a feeling of superiority, self-contempt being compensated by self-elation. This produced innumerable sub-castes in every caste, one sub-caste of Brahmins claiming superiority over others and, likewise one sub-caste of Dalits and claiming superiority over others. This developed innumerable vested interests which rendered the system invincible. Many movements sprung from within the Hindu fold to get rid of this monstrous inequity but they failed mainly because of these vested interests and secondarily because they could not and did not address economic inequality which was at the root of social and political inequality.

This was done for the first time in independent India through constitutional means of reservation and has since born considerable fruits.

Part-III

1

The Concept of 'Avatars' in Hinduism

There is no denying the fact that avatars(incarnations of God on earth-- not only in human but also in animal forms) are unique to Hinduism.They are most puzzlingfor a rationalist sympathizer who may find most of the mythology woven around them only a shade different from fairy tales. The main plank of criticism of Hinduism by Dalit and Neo-Buddhist thinkers, leftist historians and preachers of proselytizing religions (of course with an eye on conversion) have been Hindus' worship of animals as gods. And such worship becomes laughable when God is believed to have even taken 'avatar' in the form of animals— in Greek and Christian traditions, animals have no souls.

Conspicuously, all avatars are regarded to beof god Vishnu, who was one of the insignificant deities in the pantheon of Rigveda registering only a marginal presence thereas 'Upendra'--the younger brother of the heroic god Indra, givingcompany to, and drinking Soma with, him. There are just 6 Suktas (hymns)dedicated to Vishnu as against 289 to Indra and 218 to Agni, followed by Soma (123), the (group of)Vishvedevas (70), the (pair of)Aswins (56), Varuna (46), the (group of) Maruts (38),Mitra (28) and the (group of) Ushas (21) and others. With spectacular growth and popularity of Bhakti cult of Vaishnavism, Vishnulater assumed foremost position even among the three prominent Hindu deities comprising the Trinity (त्रिदेव orत्रिमूर्ति)---Brahmaa, the creator, Vishnu, the protector and Shiva, the destroyer. Before the composition of Gita (as a small part of Mahabharat—18 chapters of Bhishm Parva bunched together), Vishnu concept had well-crystallizedto confer on himan exclusive pre-eminence so as to represent the ultimate cosmic reality, the Brahman. It is Gita that provides oft-quoted rationale of the incorporeal Brahman taking corporeal avatars--यदा यदा हि धर्मस्य ग्लानिर्भवति भारत । अभ्युत्थानमधर्मस्य तदात्मानं सृजाम्यहम्॥ परित्राणाय साधूनाम् विनाशाय च दुष्कृताम्। धर्मसंस्थापनार्थाय संभवामि युगे युगे ॥ 4 :7-8 ॥ {O descendant of Bharat ! whenever there isdecline of dharma and rise of adharma, I create myself to appear for the deliverance of the pious, annihilation of the evil-doers and (thus) restoring of dharma, age after age.}

There are altogether 24 avatars, out of whom 10 are regarded as chief ones, even this short list of ten slightly varies across sects and regions. Out of these, a commonly figuring avatar of Kalki is yet to take place andis predicted to appear just before the transition from Kaliyug to Satyug in the unending time cycle of Hindus.Conspicuously, Buddha,regarded as the progenitor of Buddhist religionbut not attributed with the qualities of an avatar in themainstream Buddhism, finds a place in several versions of the list of ten avatars of Hinduism.Chronologically, Matsya (मत्स्य) viz. the Fish, Kurma (कूर्म) viz. the Tortoise, Varah (वराह) viz.the Wild Boar, Nrisimha (नृसिंह) viz.the Half Man-Half Lion, and Vaman (वामन) viz. theDwarf belong to Satyug; Parashuram (परशुराम) and Rama(राम) belong to Treta (त्रेता) ; Krishna (कृष्ण) and Balaram (who substitutes Buddha in some versions)belong toDwapar (द्वापर), leaving Buddha (बुद्ध) and yet to come Kalki (कल्कि)to belong to Kaliyug.In some Oriya literary versions,instead of Balaram , it is Jagannath and in some Maharashtrian versions, it is Vithoba who substitutes Buddha.Wherever he figures, Buddha is the last avatar having taken place and the first in Kaliyug of the present cycle of four yugas , i.e.,chaturyuga (चतुर्युग). More inclusive list of 24 includessuch names as Vyasa, Narada, Dhanvantari, Kapil (propounder of Sankhya philosophy), Dattatreya, Hayagreeva, gajendramokha, etc.

[The time span of Kaliyug is traditionally taken as 4,32,000 human years out of which only 5,116 yearsare said to have elapsed so far, leaving us in the early period of the first quarter of Kaliyug. The time span of Dwapar is said to be twice that of Kaliyug, of Treta to be thrice and of Satyug to be four times of Kaliyug, rendering the total span of one chaturyuga as43, 20,000 years. One thousand such chaturyugs constitute a day (excluding night) of Brhmaa which is known as kalpa (कल्प). After each kalpa, there is pralaya (प्रलय) i.e. dissolution followed by a state of non-existence due to absence of consciousness to cogitate the inanimate world that lasts for an equivalent period of one thousand chaturyugas comprising Brhmaa's night when he sleeps. Kalpa is divided into 14 mavantaras (मन्वंतर), each ruled by a separate Manu. By the same scale ofa 30-day month and a12-month year, the age of Brhmaa is 100 years. And Brahmaas come and go.The present kalpa is known as shvetavaaraah (श्वेतवाराह) kalpa and the present manvantera is called vaivasvata (वैवस्वत) manvantara in the name of the ruling Manu. It is believed, our Brahmaa has completed 50 years of his age and we are in the very first kalpa (Brahmaa's day)of his 51st year. It may be just coincidence that the cosmologists regard the sun of our solar system as having reached the half-way mark (five billion years) of its age (ten billion years): on the completion of rest half, its entire hydrogen and helium gases will burn away, resulting in the sun getting extinguished and all the planets with their moons; and all the comets, asteroids meteors, dwarf planets, dust and gases in the system collapsing.And there are innumerable suns (stars) with innumerable planets in our own galaxy, not to speak of the cosmos, which take birth and burn away on continuous basis. Each religious ceremony of Hindus begins with a sankalp (संकल्प), i.e. resolution, which identifies the time of the ceremony by citing all the above parameters of time beginning with the second half of the day (कल्प) of Brahmaa— 'Brahmanohni dvitiiya parardhe' (ब्रह्मणोऽह्निद्वितीय परार्धे) as also the place of the ceremony beginning with the planet earth. Hinduism with its old unbroken line does not regard creation as one-time affair, it comes into being and dissolves periodically, again and again stretching up to infinity—yatha purvamakalpayat (यथा पूर्वमकल्पयत्)—Rit Sukta (ऋत सूक्त) : 10-190. The Hindu concept of time is thus mind-boggling before merging into infinity.]

With the growing popularity of Vaishnavite cult, avatars of Rama and Krishna assumed such a great prominence in Hinduism as to become an intrinsic part of its identity whereas other avatars got marginalized. The credit mainly goes to the literary creation of Valmiki's Ramayan elaborating the story of Rama, and Bhaagavat Puranam (which being an excellent literary composition is referred to as Mahapuranam among 18 Puranas) and Mahabharata dilating on the story of Krishna. There being no proof of the historicity of the events described in these texts, Rama and Krishna can very well be said to be the creation of artistic genius of India, converting some popular tales, may be partly based on actual happenings, into almost immortal epics and, more than that, a living force, the life blood of the people of this sub-continent that they carried and spilled over Cambodia, Malaysia and Indonesia. What we call rich, multi-faceted Indian culture and civilization cannot be imagined without the software of these tales and the sustenance they provide to theday-to-day life of ordinary Indians.WhenDr. Ram Manohar Lohiya refers to Rama, Krishna and Shiva as the creation of the Indian people, a creation ofcrores of Indians through the ages and in the course of thousands of years, filling them up with the color of their dreams and their joys, he obviously refers to the compendium of thoughts, feelings and actions that these great works represent.

The mythology associated with otheravatars is scattered over several Puranas, viz., Vishnu Purana, Matsya Purana, Kuurm Purana, Varah Purana, Vaman Purana and the aforesaid Bhagavat Mahapurana. In his first avatar, by taking the form of the Fish (मत्स्यावतार), Lord Vishnu saves Manu from pralaya, carrying his boat to the freshly created world with one specimeneach of all the species of plants and animals gathered in a massive cyclone. In his second avatar, he has to take the form ofthe Tortoise (कूर्मावतार) when, in the course of churning of ocean by devas and asuras for obtaining nectar, the churning staff, mount Mandarachal (मंदराचल), started sinking and the tortoise had to bear its weight on his back. In his third avatar, he takes the form of theBoar (वराहावतार) to retrieve the earth taken away bythe demon Hiranyaksha (हिरण्याक्ष) to the bottom of the cosmic ocean, by carrying it on histusks after defeating him in a 'thousand year war'. In his fourth avatar, he takes the form of the Half man-half lion (नृसिंहावतार)to kill the demon Hiranyakashipu (हिरण्यकशिपु) , the elder brother of Hiranyaksa, who had been blessed by god Brahmaa with the immunity from being killed by a man or an animal, inside or outside the house, during day-time or night-time , with a weapon or by hand. Lord Vishnu appears from a pillar of

Hiranyakashipu's palace as nrisinha(half man, half lion) at dusk and disembowels him at the threshold of the palace, with his claws, and thereby saves his devotee and Hiranyakashipu's son Prahlad from his father'wrath. In his fifth avatar, he takes the avatar of the Dwarf (वामनावतार) to fraudulently outwit Bali(Prahlad's grandson), who had extended his dominion over the 'three words' by defeating Indra and others. Cashing in on his reputation as unparalleled donor, Vaman demands and is granted three paces of land and, by immensely extending his size, usurps the three worlds in two and a half paces, enslaving Bali in lieu of the rest half and consigning him to Patal loka with redeeming boon of immortality. Parasurama (परशुराम)placed in Treta Yug was the first avatar in the form of a normal human being. He is known as a warrior-saint and many sub-castes of Brahmins like Konkanashthas (or Chitpavans) and Bhargavas trace their origin from him. Annoyed with Kshatriya king Kartavirya for forcibly taking away the legendary cow Kamadhenu and destroying the ashrama of his father Jamadagni, he, wielding his dreaded weapon parashu (axe) in his hands, kills the king at his palace. When Kartavirya's son kills Jamadagni in revenge, he takes a vow to kill all Kshatriyas on the earth twenty-one times over, and fulfils it, filling up in the processfive lakes with their blood. He came in conflict with Rama, the other contemporary avatar of Vishnu with greater attributes (कला), but on recognizing him as such, he bowed down and left for Mahendragiri mountain for penance where he is believed to be still alive, again regarded asimmortal. Kalki is foretold to be the last avatar of this chaturyuga who will take birth in the house of a Brahmin Vishnuyash (विष्णुयश) at the fag-end of Kaliyug. Riding on his white horse, his sward drawn, he will destroy all the evils and unrighteousness and thus facilitate the transition from the dark age of Kaliyug tothe golden age of Satyug (an utopia?). The story of Rama, Krishna, Buddha and Balaram (elder brother of Krishna also regarded as the avatar of Shesha Nag— the provider of a well-protected bed to Vishnuon the milky ocean) is too well-known to require a word here.

After anxiously seeking to decipher the real significance of multiple avatars in vain, I thought it fit to refer to twoextreme views juxtaposing each other, for whatever worth they are. One view was propounded by theosophist Helena Blavatsky in her *Isis Unveiled* (1877). Reading an order of Darwinian evolution in the sequence of avatars, she finds the Fish signifying the stage of vertebrates evolved in water; the Tortoise—the stage of amphibious living in both water and land; the Boar—the stage of wild land animals; the Half man-Half lion—the stage of emergence of human thought and intelligence in powerful wild nature; the Dwarf—the stage of short, premature human beings; and Parashurama--the stage of early humans with primitive weapons living in forests. According to her, Rama reflects the stage of humans living in community and beginning of civil society, Krishna's is the stage of animal husbandry and politically advanced societies. Buddha, according to her, reaches the stage when humans find enlightenment and Kalki echoes the so-called advanced stage of humans with unimaginable power of destruction. This line was taken up by other Orientalists too. Brahmo Samaj reformer Keshab Chandra Sen (one-time teacher of Swami Vivekanand) toed this line in his attempt to harmonize traditional Hindu religion with modern science. He opines that the Avatarim of Puranas is a crude representation of the ascending scale of divine creation quite akin to the modern theory of evolution, reflecting different manifestations of the deity in different epochs of the world history, rising from the lowest scale of life to reach its perfection. Monier Williams declares that the Hindus were Darwinians centuries beforethe birth of Darwin and evolutionists before the doctrine of evolution had been accepted by the Huxleys of our time. Apart from the fact that this interpretation inverts the traditional Hindu belief of degeneration of time from Satyug to Kaliyug, a great pitfall in this obsessive overstretching is, when a 'scientific theory' is later 'scientifically'proved asincorrect, such comparisons fall flat. Social Darwinism is already under serious strain, the view gaining ascendancy that mutual cooperation and not mutual competition has been the hallmark of survival and evolution in animals as well as non-industrial human societies.

2

Jotiba Phule- Successive Aryan Invasions Disguised as Avatars

The other view with fantastic contrast comes from Jotiba Phule (1826-1890), a Dalit icon of Maharashtra and founder of Satyashodhak Samaj, now a driving force behind Dalit movementall over the country and also, to some extent, providing wherewithal for the leftist ideology concerning Indian social system. His book Gulamgiri (गुलामगीरी) (1885) written in Marathi with English Introduction constitutes the most powerful and ruthless indictment of Hindu Avatarism, rather Hinduism as such. Phule presented a sharp antithesis of European 'Orientalists' who saw the Vedas as an ancient spiritual link between Europeans and Indians, thus turning Orientalism on its head. In avatars, he foundforging of a deceitfulmythology by cruel and wilyBrahmins, *'Irani Arya-bhats'* (*ईरानी आर्य भट*), to disguise their violent invasion of India from Iran, upsetting an originally prosperous and egalitarian society of aboriginals whom they termed as Rakshasa, Asura, Shudra (according to Phule derived from the word Kshudra–क्षुद्र) and Atishudra (dalit). Phuleregards Rakshasa as rakshaka(रक्षक) of the people, asura as shura (शूर-valliant) and Atishudra as the hero of the people: Atishudras fought Brahmin domination more fiercely than the Shudras and hence were subjected to greater oppression out of revenge, downgrading them to the lowest level of untouchables in the caste hierarchy. According to Phule, it is in order to solidify their rule or ʻbhatshahiʼ *(भटशाही)*ʼ,that a religious ideology based onBrahmin hegemony, inequality by birth and perpetual exploitation and oppression was constructed in the Puranas and avatarism was an intrinsic part of the same.

Regarding different avatars of Vishnu, Phule holds them to represent the stages in which the country was conquered by Brahmin or Aryan invaders from Iran. He explains Matsyavatar with reference to Aryan invasion through sea-route on small boats crossing water surface swiftly like fish, which gave the nickname Matsya (मत्स्य) to the leader of theinvading Aryan tribe. They landed at a port on the western sea and killed the local chieftain Shankhasur (शंखासुर), taking over his dominion, which remained with Aryanstill Matsya's death. Thereafter, Shankhasur's menmade a vigorous attackto recover their possessions and defeated the Aryans, whofled and took to hiding in a forest atop a hillock near the sea-port. It so happened that at that very juncture, another and bigger tribe of Aryans from Iran reached thesea-port. Being in larger number, they were moving slowly on the water like tortoise and hence their chief was called Kachchhap (कच्छप). They first took possession of the one-side slope of the hillock driving out Shankhasur's men from there. The aboriginals regrouped under their new chief Kashyap(कश्यप).The Aryans under Kachchhap descended down the slope, keeping the hillock ontheir back, fighting so hard as not to yield their position till the last (parallel to Puranic story of Kachchhap holding Manadarachal mountain stable on his back?).Then came the Aryan chief Varah who was so clumsy and dirty in his habits, conduct and living and so quick in pouncing on his opponents that the two great warriors of the aboriginals, Hiranyaksha and Hiranyakashipu, called him a pig (sukar—सूकर or varah) out of contempt. Infuriated at this insult, Varah attacked their provinces again and again, torturing the inhabitants to the extreme. In one of the fights, he killed Hiranyaksha. But soon he also died. Then came Nrisinha. Unable to subdue Hiranyakashipu in open battle, he intrigued with his son, Prahlad (प्रह्लाद), by brainwashing him and making him shun the worship of his family deity, Harahar. Nrisnha then instigated Prahlad to kill his father but the latter could not dare. Then he conspired with Prahlad to neutralize Hiranyakashipu's plans ofresistance and, at an opportune moment, entered his palace with Prahlad's help, disguised as a lion and wrapping the disguise with a sari in the style of a coquettish woman with a big veil, and hid behind a pillar. When Hiranyakashipu returned from his daily work to take rest, Nrisinha, removing his veil and tying the sari around his waist, pounced on him and killed him with lion's nail that he had hidden in his palms. Thereupon, he deserted the place with all the Brahmins and went back to his country. Only then Prahlad could realize that he was diched and he along with his people started calling Brahmins vipriya (विप्रिय in Marathi, meaningcheat) which later became Vipra (विप्र, i.e., ब्राह्मण). After Prahlad, his son, Virochan (विरोचन), and then his grandson, Bali (बलि), became the ruler. Bali was an outstandingly able, just and popular ruler as also a valiant fighter; he extended his dominion overseveral neighboring provinces by liberating them from the yoke of Aryan invaders. At that time,Vaman, the dwarf, was the chief of the Aryans. He mobilized a huge army, crossed the frontiers of Bali'dominions and, unleashinga reign of terror and devastation on his way, reached Bali's capital so swiftly that the later was left with no time to organize defense by collecting his chieftains with their forces whom he had given a call. Despite this, he valiantly fought against Vaman's forces for nearly a month and was killed. On hearing the news, his wife Vindhyavali (विंध्यावली), burnt herself in a fire-pit out of grief, thus initiating the custom of Sati. His son, Vanasur (वाणासुर) had to flee after a further day-long battle, leaving the capital exposed for plunder of immense gold and riches stocked there. But soon the chieftains called by Bali turned up with their contingents adding great strength to Vanasur's force, whereupon he invaded, defeated and plundered the Brahmin camp, taking back all the wealth they had looted, and pursued them when they fled towards Himalayas. There he laid siege at the approach of the hill they had taken shelter on and starved them including Vamana to death.

In support of Bali's beneficence and popularity as a peasant king, Phule cites the Marathi saying '*ida pida javo, balica rajya yaevo*' (let troubles and sorrows go and the kingdom of Bali come) still in vogue, andmany customs, rituals and festivals observed among non-Brahmins in Maharshtra commemorating Bali'spopular rule. He refers to several non-Vedic gods having non-Brahmin priests (except Vithoba who was usurped by Brahmins by including him in the ten avatars) who still continue to be worshipped from pre-Aryan golden era.

After the death of Vaman, in that state of duress under siege there being no time to appoint a new leader, it was left to the clever officemanager Prajapita(Brahmaa)to handle all the affairs of the Aryans. He was so unreliable that people started calling him chaturmukh(चतुर्मुख)—the one indulging not only in double but quadruple talk. It is he who discovered the device of writing on dry palm leaves with a pointed stick. All that these invaders remembered of the meaningless, insipidstories from Iran full ofmagic and miracles were reduced to writing in Persian-style small meter poems (श्लोकs) in the then prevalent Sanskrit language, by mixing some other stories of their own. But due to starvation under the siege laid by Banasur, many of the Aryans fled back to Iran and those left could surviveby killing and eating their horses and other animals, giving the honorific name of Ashvamedha Yajna to this act of killing. Later, when Vanasur died (apparently issue-less or with no surviving issue), there was total chaos and disorder. Taking advantage, hungry, starving and desperate Brahmins led by Brhmaa attacked the aboriginals during night and captured all their possessions, enslaving them and converting them into shudras. The sections of the aboriginals fighting with greatest fervor weretermed as Maha-ari (great enemy) which later became Mahar, a dalit caste of Maharashtra (which was recognized as a martial caste for induction in the armed forcesby the British and in which Dr. Ambedkar was born).

But Phule had reserved his most hateful narrative for Prashuram, who became chief of Brahmins after the death of Brahmaa. His was the period when total and extensive defeat and subjugation of the fighting force of aboriginals who were Kshatriyas (Maha-aries) and the consolidation of Brahmin rule was completed.[To Phule, Kshatriyas were not Aryans but aboriginals (same as Shudras or backward)-- this position corresponds with the Maharashtrian social structure where Brahmins alone constitutethe caste Hindus, leaving shudras (backwards) and atishudras (dalits, earlier untouchables) whom Phule regarded as aboriginals. In Phule's own words, 'Parashuram was, by nature, troublesome, courageous, destructive, cruel, foolish and of evil disposition' He was 'physically strong and a good archer'. At the instructions of his father, he beheaded his mother Renuka. [Puranas redeem this crime with the story that Parashuram did it at the command of his father, who was annoyed with Renuka on account of her failure to bring water (due to breaking of earthen pitcher), but when Parashuram showed such extreme obedience, he was pleased to offer a boon of his choice and Parashuram demanded his mother's resurrection, which was granted and she became alive.]In Parashuram's time, Maha-aries attacked the Aryan establishments 21 times to liberate their enslaved brethren and fought with such determination that they were called dwaiti (in Marathi, meaning obstinate) that later became daitya (दैत्य).They were ultimately crushed and, losing all hope, many of them fled and hid in lower Konkan region to spend their last days. Those who were captured were forced to take a vow that they will never revolt against Brahmins and for their identification a black thread was tied around their neck and even other shudras for whose liberation they had fought were forbidden to touch them. That is how the class of untouchables or atishudras or Pancham Varana came into being. In this long-drawn war so many lives were lost on Parashuram's side too that Brahmins got annoyed with him. Coupled with this, he was badly defeated by one of the chieftains' son, Ramachandra, who had broken his bow. Humiliated and ashamed, Parashuram left the kingdom and took abode in lower Konkan region to atone for his sins. There he died at an unknown spot and unknown time, enablingsuperstitious Brahmins to regard him as immortal and an avatar of Aadinarayan (आदिनारायण). {Chapters 2 to 8 of Gulamgiri summarized from Hindi translation by Dr. Vimalkirti.}

Jotiba Bhule is acclaimed as a rationalist thinker, reformer and activist of nineteenth century who worked incessantly for the upliftment of dalits, backwards and women and rendered yeomen service for the education of women. Born in to-day's 'affluent OBC' caste of Mali, the gardener, which is classed with Maratha Kunbies as people of middle status,he began working on his pioneering mission by establishing schools for both girls and untouchable boys. He wrote many plays and poems including a ballad on Shivaji, and three polemical works attacking Brahmanism—*Gulamgiri, Setkaryaca Asud* (Oppression of the Peasants) and *Satya Dharma*(True Religion).Dr. Ambedkar acknowledged him as one of his 'gurus' although very little of Phule's influence is seen in his writings.

No doubt, caste-discrimination traditionally practiced inHindu society and particularly the cruel, inhuman treatment meted out to the untouchables is abhorring. It is worth pondering how the vested interests mainly from among the Brahmins orchestrated and fortified this hazardous practice of inequality by birth, vesting umpteen privileges on a few and horrific disadvantages on the rest, that lasted for thousands of years—there is absolutely no trace of casteism in Rigveda . But there is much to be desired in Phule's critique of Hinduism in general and avatarism in particular too. It is not based on the basic tenets of humanism—intrinsic equality and dignity of all men and progress with mutual cooperation and not exploitation of one by the other. Instead, it deconstructs the unscientific Puranic version imbibed, by his own reckoning, in meaningless stories, to replace it by equally unscientific and unhistorical narrative of racial conflict by taking clue from some titbits and loose ends of those very Puranic stories and seeking support from some selected customs and rituals among non-Brahmin population of Maharashtra and some other pockets. In the process, it builds a theory based on hatred to counter another theory based on hatred, which never works—mud can never be washed by mud. Secondly, Phule's narrative is Maharashtra-centric, it takes in and subsumes relevant Puranic themes to interpret them in the context of Maharashtra, seeking support from the sayings, customs and rituals prevalent there. In the process, Maharashtra throws up an arena for not only Bali but also Aryan invasion (migration?), Varah, Vaman, Parashuram, Ramachandra (of Ayodhya) and even the origin of Sati, the last one must be at great consternation of many Dalit activists who unceasingly slight caste Hindus for their cruel practice of Sati, which is historically associated with caste Hindus of Rajasthan and Bengal, whereas Phule traces its origin to the wife of aboriginal king Bali of Maharashtra. These geographical confines for a complex all-India phenomenon render the narrative quite unhistorical. Thirdly, without any discussion of the alternative theories, Phule bluntly presumes Aryan migration from Iran to Maharashtra through sea-route, cutting at the root of generally accepted theory of Aryan migration from Central Asia by land route, branching out to Europe, Iran and India, the Indian branch naturally entering from north-westand moving south-east—they must have reached Maharashtra quite late. When Phule talks of Aryan invasion on Maharashtra by sea-route from Iran (Persia), he never implies that the invaders were originally from Central Asia and had made Iran their home by another invasion earlier.

After going carefully through the western theory of Aryan migration and Aryan-Dravidian conflict believed by many of us including Pt. Nehru, I, for one, have failed to find any clinching or convincing evidence in support—just imagination running amok on the basis of some scanty material of doubtful nature. Migration of Homo sapiens all over the world probably beginning from Africa may be a pre-historic phenomenon and cannot be commissioned to support a racial theory for the origin of caste-system in India. Dr. Ambedkar in his monograph 'Annihilation of Caste' opines: *"As a matter of fact Caste system came into being long after the different races of India had co-mingled in blood and culture. To hold that distinctions of Caste are really distinctions of race and treat different Castes as though they were so many different races is a gross perversion of facts. What racial affinity is there between the Brahmin of the Punjab and the Brahmin of Madras? What racial affinity is there between the untouchable of Bengal and the untouchable of Madras? What racial difference is there between the Brahmin of the Punjab and the Chamar of the Punjab? What racial difference is there between the Brahmin of Madras and the pariah of Madras? The Brahmin of the Punjab is racially of the same stock as the Chamar of the Punjab and the Brahmin of Madras is of the same race as the Pariah of Madras. Caste system does not demarcate racial division. Caste system is a social division of the people of the same race."* How is it that such a vast ancient Hindu literature beginning with Rigveda and encompassing Shruties (Vedas, Brahmanas, Aranyakas, Upanishads, Vedangas and Sutra-granthas), Smrities, Puranas, 'Itihasa'-granths of Ramayan and Mahabharata, Agamas (Tantrashastra) and those on Philosophy, Grammar, Poetics, Astrology, Ayurveda and innumerable literary works in prose, poetry, Champu and Natak are bereft the memories of the terrain, the rivers, the mountains and the valleys of the erstwhile land of the 'Aryans'—had their nostalgic memories were totally wiped off? Just one question out of many. Why didn't this happen with the Indians living in Fiji, Mauritius, Guyana, Surinam, Trinidad and Tobago? They still remember with longing what we have already forgotten. And there are umpteen cities in the US that bear the same name as the cities of England with the epithet 'New', so much so that there is a region named New England. Such an all-pervading, successful conspiracy among 'Aryans' to forget or not to mention? Unbelievable.

This swinging to the other extreme by Phule perhaps explains the fact that, although his denigration of avatarism as part of inversion of Orientalism impacted many Dalit scholars and activists like Gail Omvedt and also influenced the leftist school of historiography represented by suchicons as Romila Thapar, it left no impact on the actual behavior of masses. The Dalit and backward empowerment in India had to wait for actualization of relevant constitutional provisions. Even there, the parties coming to power on that plank soon lost their direction and imbibed the vices of the mainstream political class. Now they are struggling to survive by extending their base from Bahujan Samaj to Sarvajan Samaj or making opportunistic coalitions. There is a limit to the ideas influencing human behavior.

Is it not the time to introspect on this hate-centric ideology and strive for rational, objective and dispassionately balanced historical approach?

3

Philosophical Basis of Hinduism

The first part of the article began with the proposition that Hinduism is not a religion in the sense of the term asused in English language. The origin of the word 'religion' in English is traced back to the Latin words 'religare' (verb) and 'religio' (noun) meaning 'to re-bind' and 're-binding' (obligation, bond, reverence) respectively. So, religion is that which re-binds one with God and through him with others. Romans as also Greeks practiced polytheism like Hindus, worshipping different gods with different attributes of nature. Hence, for them religion was a bond with, an obligation to, and a reverence for, multiple gods. In monotheistic Christianity it became bond, obligation and reverence for a personal God and His son, the Prophet.

In Islam Mazahab (मज़हब) is an Arabic word which means belief, faith, trust in a single personal God without any doubt. Later it came to denote different sects based on interpretation of Sharia by different schools of Islamic law or jurisprudence (Fiqh). These schools—Hanafi, Maliki, Shafi, Hanbali, Zahiri and Jariri (since extinct) of Sunni sect; Ismaili, Jafari and Zaidi of Shia sect; and Ibadi of other than Sunni and Shia sects--developed within 150 years or so of the journey of Islam.

In Hinduism, Dharma (धर्म) as equivalent to earlier term Rit (ऋत) with its origin in hoary past has unique connotation as distinct from 'religion' in Christianity and 'Mazahab' in Islam. It is a universal, eternal and purely secular concept, being close to primordial truth sustaining and governing the universe and all its constituents including mankind. This has more of a philosophical than religious connotation. It is somewhat akin to 'Natural Law' of Heraclitus (540 BC-480 BC), the renowned philosopher of ancient Greece.

The earliest available compilation of Hindu philosophy which shaped their way of life and world view is Rigveda followed by Yajurveda, Samveda and Atharvaved respectively. Rigveda is divided into ten books each containing varying number of hymns (Suktas) composed by different Rishis and each hymn comprises varying number of verses (Richas or Mantras). The total number of Suktas in Rigved is 1048 consisting of altogether10, 600 Richas. These Suktas are in praise of different gods representing different attributes of nature but they also contain certain mythological stories and discourses on fundamental philosophical questions of creation and existence. Samaveda is mainly a collection of lyrical hymns from Rigveda which were sung with a typical accent and style by specially trained singers called उद्गाता (Udgata). Yajurveda is available in two versions of two different शाखा (schools) called Shukla (White) and Krishna (Black) and contains certain Mantras of Rigveda and Atharvaveda. It deals with different Yajnas, their methods and rituals and the fruits of their performance. Atharvaveda deals with miscellaneous subjects like diseases and their treatment, ceremonies like those performed on birth, marriage and death etc. besides war craft, magic, sorcery and witchcraft. Then there are Brahman works elaborating the rituals of yajnas, and Upanishads dealing with the knowledge of ultimate on the basis of interpretation of Vedas.

Despite containing hymns in praise of different gods representing different aspects of nature, the concept of ultimate reality being one permeates entire Rigved. The following Richa bears ample testimony of the concept of this oneness behind the multiplicity of nature's forces represented by different gods—

इन्द्रं मित्रं वरुणमग्निमाहुरथो स दिव्यो सुपर्णो गरुत्मान्।

एकं सद्विप्रा बहुधा वदंति अग्निं यमं मातरिश्वानमाहु: ॥

(ऋग्वेद, 1:164.46)

[That (truth or supreme reality) is one. The knowledgeable call him by different names—Indra, Mitra, Varun, Agni, the celestial Garud of beautiful wings, Yama and Matarishvan, etc.]

This spirit of catholicity imbibed in Rigveda runs through the entire tradition of Hinduism encompassing the Samhitas, Brahmanas, Aranyakas, Upnishads, Sutras, Smritis, Puranas and even literary works of epics, poetry and plays. Much later, when the Rigvedic philosophy and pantheon is well stratified, incorporating six schools of philosophy and the concept of Avatars, a beautiful verse of Hanumannaatakam echoes the same spirit—

यं शैवा: समुपासते शिव इति ब्रह्मेति वेदांतिनोबौद्धा बुद्ध इति प्रमाणपटव: कर्तेति नैयायिका:।

अहन्नित्यथ जैनशासनरता: कर्मेति मीमांसका: सोऽयं वो विदधातु वाञ्छितफलं त्रैलोक्यनाथो हरि:॥

[The one who is worshipped as Shiva by Shaivas, as Brahman by Vedantis, as

Budddha by Buddhists, as Karta by logically well-skilled Naiyayikas, as Arhan by the followers of Jain discipline and as Karma by Mimansakas, the same Vishnu, the Lord of the three Lokas, may fructify all my desired fruits.]

The essence of Hinduism lies in the six schools of Vedic philosophy that flourished during Sutra period (after Buddha). All these six schools claim to be based on Vedas, Brahmans and Upanishads. These can be divided into two categories: those concerning knowledge of being (ज्ञानकांड of Vedas) and those concerning yajnas and rituals (कर्मकांड of Vedas). In the first category are Nyaya school founded by Gautam (Nyaya-Sutra), Vaisheshik School founded by Kanad (Vaisheshik-Sutra), Sankhya School founded by Kapil (Sankhya-Sutra), Yoga School founded by Patanjali (Yogasutra) and Vedanta School founded by Badarayan (Brahmasutra). In the second category falls Mimansa School alone, which was founded by Jaimini and derives authority from Jaimini Sutra. Ironically, it is only Mimansa School of philosophy with its concepts of polytheism, fruits of one's deeds (कर्मफल), rebirth, heaven and hell, and the Bhakti cult derived from Puranic mythology that chiefly govern day-to-day religious life of present-day Hindus.

4

Six Schools of Vedic Philosophy

Nyaya (न्याय)

This School of Gautam (गौतम) strives to prove the divine by logic on the basis of proofs—direct experience, inferences and parallels drawn from such experiences and reliable words of Vedas which constitute its epistemology. It aims to liberate the soul, which is not limited by time and space, from the bondage of body and the cycle of birth and death, which are the result of our deeds that bear fruits in accordance with the rule of cause and effect and produce pleasure and pain. Cumulative effect of our earlier deeds, good or bad, creates what is called Adrishta which bears fruits in future and hence the correlation between the deeds and the fruits is not always visible. Since this Adrishta is unconscious and inert, there has to be a power to regulate it and that power is God. But God cannot violate the correlation between the deeds and the fruits, he is thus reduced to a mere accountant, so to say.

Vaisheshik (वैशेषिक)

This School ofKanad (कणाद) is a sister school of Nyaya and follows former's postulates in many respects, particularly in regard to the concept of God and liberation (अपवर्ग). But what is peculiar to Vaishashik is its naturalist approach towards matter and motion. In Kanad's philosophy physics is central to understanding of the universe. He asserts that all substances are ultimately composed of atoms (परमाणु), being the smallest particle which subsists by combining together to form molecule (अणु). He holds the view that atoms are eternal, they cannot be created nor can be destroyed. He classifies all substances into seven categories— matter (द्रव्य), quality (गुण), activity

(कर्म), generality (सामान्य), particularity (विशेष) (hence the name Vaisheshik), inherence (समवाय), and absence (अभाव). He enumerates nine categories of matter (द्रव्य)--earth (क्षिति), water (जल), fire (अग्नि), air (वायु), space (आकाश), time (काल), direction (दिक्), soul (आत्मा), and mind(मन). Out of these, space, direction and time are unique in that they are invisible, eternal and all-pervading (विभु). But Kanad's atomism differs from western materialist atomism inasmuch as in the latter there is automation in the motion of atoms, there being no conscious entity to regulate the same. On the other hand, in Kanad, it is the divine force that regulates the motion of atoms. This divine force, like that in Nyaya philosophy, ensures the fruits of living beings' karma to materialize through Adrishta and also causes creation and its dissolution (प्रलय) to happen.

Sankhya (सांख्य)

The basic characteristic of Sankhya philosophy of Kapil is dualism and atheism. The creation according to Kapil is the effect of interaction between the two elements of universe--Purush, the consciousness, and Prakriti (nature), the unconscious matter--without there being any divine role therein. Prakriti has three qualities (गुण)—Satva, Raj and Tam. Satva represents goodness, compassion and positivity; Raj represents activity, passion and impulsiveness, whereas Tam represents darkness, ignorance, laziness and negativity. Nature with these three qualities is primeval cause of creation. There is no cause of nature, it is eternal though ever changing. It remains unmanifested as long as the three Gunas are in equilibrium. It is the interplay of these Gunas that defines the character of someone or something. Sankhya enumerates altogether 25 elements, hence the name Sankhya.

These are five perceptions (तन्मात्र)-- sound, feeling of touch (tangability), form, taste and smell; five sense organs; five work organs; five elements (महाभूत)—earth, water, fire, air and space; mind (मन); intellect (महत्); egotism (अहंकार); soul (आत्मा);and Purush who is pure consciousness and enjoyer (भोक्ता) of enjoyable (भोग्य) Prakriti. Except for Purush, the rest 24 elements are within Prakriti. Thus, unlike Descarte's dualism of body and mind, Kapil's dualism is between Prakriti comprising both body and mind and Purush (pure consciousness.

According to Kapil, the Vedas refer only to Prakriti and not to God. He gives elaborate reasons for rejecting the concept of God—

--If the existence of karma is assumed, the proposition of God as a moral governor of the universe is unnecessary. For, if God can enforce the consequences of actions then he can do so even without karma of the subjects. If, however, he is assumed to be within the law of karma, then karma itself would be the giver of consequences and there would be no need of a God.

--Even if karma is denied, God still cannot be the enforcer of consequences. Because the motives of an enforcer God would be either egoistic or altruistic. God's motives cannot be assumed to be altruistic because an altruistic God would not create a world so full of suffering. If his motives are assumed to be egoistic, then God must be thought to have desire, as agency or authority cannot be established in the absence of desire. However, if it is assumed that the God possesses desires that would contradict God's eternal freedom which necessitates no compulsion in actions. Moreover, desire, according to Samkhya, is an attribute of Prakṛiti and cannot be thought to grow in God. The testimony of the Vedas, according to Samkhya, also confirms this notion.

--Despite arguments to the contrary, if God is still assumed to possess unfulfilled desires, this would cause him to suffer pain and other similar human experiences. Such a worldly God would be no better than Samkhya's notion of higher self (Purush).

--There is no proof of the existence of God. He is not the object of perception, there exists no general proposition that can prove him by inference. And the Vedas speak of

Prakṛti as the origin of the universe, not God.

Samkhya philosophy accordingly maintains that the various cosmological, ontological and teleological arguments cannot prove the existence of God.

Kapil's is a Vedic philosophy adhering to Vedic texts but taking not only atheist line but also giving tangible reasons for the same. It is noteworthy that, out of the progenitors of six schools of Vedic philosophy, only Kapil was later accorded the status of an Avatar of Vishnu being one of his twenty four Avatars (Bhagavat, Narad, Brahmand, Vishnu, Padma and Skanda Puranas, Vishnusahasranam and Valmiki Ramayana). That is but an irrefutable proof of highest degree of eclecticism in Vedic philosophical tradition running down from Rigveda. And Hindu Dharma is one with Vedic philosophy at least in theory.

Yoga (योग)

Yoga philosophy of Patanjali is complementary to Sankhya philosophy of Kapil. It has the same goal of Kaivalya, the realization of one's self, that is, pure consciousness, by being free from the shackles of nature. Patanjali's Yogsutra provides a roadmap for this realization through Yam, Niyam, Asan, Pranayam, Pratyahar, Dharana, Dhyan and Samadhi, the eight limbs of Yoga. In fact, this roadmap is valid for all the six schools of Vedic philosophy in one way or the other. Yoga is thus not mere Asanas or poses of body which have more to do with Hathayoga than Patanjal Yoga. As defined in Yogasutra, Asana is merely a pose of sitting steadily and comfortably (स्थिर सुखमासनम्‌–योगसूत्र 2: 46).

The only vital difference between Kapil and Pantajali is regarding divine concept. Whereas Kapil rejects the divine concept by giving elaborate reasons, Patanjali takes God as a given and neither answers the objections of Kapil nor gives any positive argument to establish Him. It is noteworthy that Patanjali does not treat God as the cause of creation nor indispensable for realization of the goal of life, that is, Kaivalya through Yoga. The reference of God (ईश्वर) occurs only in seven Sutras of Yogasutra (1: 23-29). The context is how to obtain the state of Asamprajnayat Samadhi (असंप्रज्ञात समाधि)

which purifies the mind to enable one to reach Kaivalya. It is said, it requires faith, virility, memory, and Samadhi in the ascending order (1:20). And this process is accelerated when the will (संवेग) is strong. Alternatively, Patanjali ordains, it can also be accelerated by surrendering to God (ईश्वरप्रणिधानाद्वा—1:23). It is in this context that Patanjali describes the qualities of God. He is omniscient (तत्र निरतिशयं सर्वज्ञबीजम्—1:25). He, not being limited by time, is also the teacher of ancestors (पूर्वेषामपि गुरु: कालेनानवच्छेदात्--1:26). He is called Pranav—Omkar (ॐ कार) (तस्य वाचक: प्रणव:--1:27). One should mutter Omkar and ponder over its meaning (तज्जपस्तदर्थभावनम्--1:28). From this the impediments are removed and one also realizes his inner self (तत: प्रत्यक्चेतनाधिगमोऽप्यंतरायाभावश्च—1:29).

And that's all so far as God is concerned. Thus, Patalaji's Yogasutra does not grant God the pre-eminence of creator, sustainer and destroyer of the world and regulator of Karmaphal. Despite being called Seshwar Sankhya, Yog philosophy does not make a break from the premises of Sankhya and confines itself to only a lip service

to God as an alternative to strong
will for the speedy achievement of
Asamprajnyat Samadhi to realize the
goal of life.

Mimansa (मीमांसा)

Mimansa of Jaimini (also called
Purvamimansa in the context of
Uttarmimansa, that is, Vedanta) is, as
stated above, the only school of Vedic
philosophy that relies on Karma Kand
of Vedas. Another peculiarity of this
school is, like Sankhya, what it
propounds is clearly an atheist
philosophy despite strictly adhering
to Vedic texts.

Entire Vedic literature except
Upnishads deals with dharma as acts of
duty, of which the chief are Yajnas.
Even Shankar propounding Adyait Vedant
(at peak of Jnana Kand) insists on
sacred rites being necessary for
realization of jnana as a fruit of
karma of this or earlier life. Mimansa
means discussion on the doubts as to
what really a thing or a phenomenon
is. Mimansa of rules of rituals
regarding yajnas and samsakaras began
in the Vedic period itself. Many
problems regarding interpretation of
rules were discussed and decided as
they arose. These decisions are

scattered in the Brahman works but they are disjointed, obscure and incomplete and cannot be resolved without oral help which was then available in the oral tradition. Vedic texts and oral traditions continued for a long time as two authorities on performance of religious duties of Yajnas and Samskaras which gave rise to different Vedic Shakhas (schools). After the rise of Buddhism the followers were called upon to review and recast all the material of texts and oral tradition that they possessed to prove its soundness. This was the background in which Jaimini attempted the work of systematizing the rules of Mimansa in Sutra (aphorism) form and compiling them in his Jaimini Sutra.

Accordingly, the purpose of this school is practical elucidation of rituals than philosophical discourse which is subordinate to the former. In the scheme of things it affirms the reality of the soul and regards it as permanent being possessing the body to which the results of ritualistic acts accrue. The authority for the character of these acts as dharma and their ability to produce beneficial results lies in Vedas which do not need any other authority to rest upon. But when other thinkers of the time were disparaging Vedic texts, such dogmatic view would not work. Hence, Mimansa also attempts to elaborate its philosophical position but it welcomes other philosophical positions so long as they do not question its central theme of transcendent importance of dharma as imbibed in Vedas in ritualistic terms. Mimansa acknowledges Vedas as authoritative as against the Buddhists who dispute it and also against those who subordinate karma to jnana. Like Vedas, Mimansa is polytheistic. But its implication is not theistic but atheistic where following the prescriptions and restrictions prescribed in the Vedas is the only dharma that sets the goal of life. Jaimini regards the universe as eternal without there being need of creation and its dissolution. Hence, there is no rationale of God. According to Jaimini, the relation between words (शब्द) and their meanings (अर्थ) is eternal and Vedas being Apaurusheya (अपौरुषेय), they are the eternal source of knowledge and Dharma. One should perform what is prescribed in Vedas without desire of its fruits which will destroy the ill fruits of previous karmas and ensure liberation. According to Mimansa, performance of yajnas etc prescribed in Vedas creates phenomenal merit which it calls Apurva (अपूर्व) that yield fruits at appropriate time either in this life or afterlife. Mimansa thus takes a realistic view of the world as against the Buddhists. Modern Hindu law is considerably influenced by the Mimansa system.

Vedanta (वेदांत)

Ultimately all the five Schools of Vedic philosophy culminated into Vedanta School which relies on Jnana Kand of Vedic literature that flourished in Upnishads. The philosophy of this school was systematized in Brahma Sutra (also called Vedanta Sutra) by Badrayan. Some scholars identify Badrayan with Krishnadyaipayan Vyas. Shankar, Ramanuj, Vallabh and other Acharyas have written detailed commentaries on Brahma Sutra wherein Shankar's commentary is regarded as the most authentic.

Vedanta philosophy of Shankar is absolute monism which means, the ultimate reality is one that permeates the universe. This ultimate reality is Atman or supreme consciousness. The visible universe is Maya (the play), only a shadow of that supreme consciousness. Both Atman and Maya have no beginning but Atman has no end as well, whereas one can get rid of Maya by realizing Atman. The individual soul is not different or distinct from atman, it is only its reflection shrouded by Maya. Liberation from Maya consists in realization of oneness of the individual soul with the absolute soul. And that is a state of pure bliss unlike the liberation of Nyaya which is only absence of pleasure and pain which are so mixed up that one cannot have pleasure alone. According to Vedanta, the visible universe is not unreal, it is also an integral part of Atman or Brahman but it is perishable and hence it constitutes an intermediate entity between being and non-being. The finite individuals cannot normally imagine the infinite atman without limiting it. But the goal or the ideal of life, remains the same, that is, realization of oneness. When that happens, the knower, the known and the knowledge (ज्ञाता, ज्ञेय, ज्ञान) become one.

Shankar accepted the Varna and caste systems of social organization but held that any person belonging to any caste could attain the highest knowledge and obtain liberation, a poor respite however. He travelled from South to North, East and West, to every corner of the country, meeting people, arguing, debating, reasoning, convincing and filling them with a part of his own passion and vitality. He is said to have established four great Mathas locating them almost at the four corners of India—Shringeri in Mysore, Puri on the east coast, Dvaraka on the west coast and Badrinath in the north in the heart of Himalayas. Shankar is said to have helped in putting an end to Buddhism in India. But Buddhism had shrunk in India even before Shankar. Brahmanism rather absorbed it in a fraternal embrace. Shankar's monistic philosophy devoid of personal God makes his opponents call him a disguised Buddhist (प्रच्छन्न बौद्ध).

As pointed out earlier, modern Hindu religious and social life is dominated by expensive ceremonies, rites and rituals with a lot of fanfare and without understanding any meaning and significance thereof, just as a matter of social prestige. Out of the six schools of Vedic philosophy, Mimansa rules the roost in that sense.

5

Birth of Bhakti Cult and Its Implications

It is almost settled that Bhakti cult arose in Tamil Nadu in the form of devotional songs composed by saint-poets Alvar (आलवार) between fifth and tenth centuries although the orthodox tradition places them far more earlier, ie, 4200-2700 BC. Their number was traditionally considered to be ten but two more names of Andal (a woman saint) and Madhurkavi (मधुरकवि) were added later on the basis of some additional references found, making it twelve. Alvars espouse the cause of devotion to Lord Vishnu (an insignificant deity in Rigvedic pantheon) and express love, longing and devotion to him as Supreme deity with ecstasy. Their songs reflect depth of feeling and felicity of expression that contributed to growth of Vaishnavism independent of Sanskrit and ritualistic Vedic tradition.

In fact, a parallel folk tradition of Lokayatas is traceable to pre-Buddhist and even pre-Upanishad period which was referred to as Asur-view or Dehavad (देहवाद). The names of at least three of its proponents are readily available—Brihaspati (बृहस्पति) Pushpadant (पुष्पदंत) and Jabali (जाबालि). Etymologically, Lokayata means 'that which is prevalent among the people' and also 'that which is essentially this-worldly'. It can be inferred that this strand of Indian philosophy would have been popular among the masses. On philosophical plane it is opposed to the conceptions of God, soul and otherworld. According to Dehavad, material human body is the microcosm of the universe whose birth is the result of similar processes as the birth of human beings. This view might have survived in matriarchal tribal societies and later turned into Tantrism with its obscure and obscene rituals and supreme emphasis on female principle called the Shakti or Prakriti which persisted along with the advanced and civilized societies. The account of Lokayata philosophy as available in Sarva Darshan Sangraha (Compendium of Indian Philosophy) of Madhavacharya (13th -14th Century) cannot be taken on its face value,

Madhava being staunch protagonist of theistic philosophy of Dualism. There still is a chaotic presence of many parallel traditions of strange rituals including ghost worship in particular castes, tribes and other groups in different parts of the country. They represent subaltern prototypes of Hindu practices and cannot be treated as counter to mainstream Hindu philosophy. Debi Prasad Chattopadhyaay in his book 'Lokayyata: A study of Anciant Indian Materialism' has taken great pains to reconstruct Lokayata philosophy with the help of sporadic references in Upanishads and other texts. But he has no answer to ethical bankruptcy and negativity irresistibly arising from absolute materialism of Lokayats. On the other hand, Alvar saints, as earliest protagonists of egalitarian Bhakti cult with due emphasis on piety and morality in life, present a non-Sanskrit, non-Vedic tradition of common people as a shining example of pluralist folk tradition of India in contrast with elitist voice of Vedic philosophy.

However, the philosophical foundation of Bhakti cult was left to be laid down by Ramanuj (1017- 1137 AD) who came after Shankar (788-820 AD) from the same tradition of Vedantic monasteries with a new construct of Vishishtadvait (विशिष्टाद्वैत) by qualifying Shankar's Advaita. According to Ramanuj, both conscious atman and unconscious matter are the constituents of supreme reality, i.e, omnipotent God as both are eternal and are governed by Him. The creation is not merely a shadow or play (माया) but real, both the snake and the rope are true, the confusion arises on account of similarity of two real things and not one of the two being unreal. In his commentary (श्री भाष्य) on Brahma Sutra, Ramanuj counters Shankar's Mayavad with the argument that Atman or Braman is pure consciousness and by nature self-illuminative. If it is contended that He can be shrouded by ignorance (अविद्या) on account of Maya, that amounts to saying that Maya can destroy the nature of Brahman. The fact is that Brahman is both conscious living being and inert nature as there is no existence of any phenomenon other than, and independent of, Brahman. On account of being both conscious being and unconscious nature, He is one with the both but, at the same time, special for both, hence the nomenclature विशिष्टाद्वैत. According to Ramanuj, mere knowledge of Vedanta cannot lead to deliverance.

Real knowledge lies in constant remembrance of, and complete surrender before, God. And that is what is called Bhakti or Upasana (उपासना). This is also the ultimate means of liberation from the cycle of birth and death as it destroys not only ignorance but also the Karmas which cause our birth.

Thus, Ramanuj turns Shankar's Monism upside down, making the God not a state of man's enlightened consciousness but a lord who needs man's complete surrender like a slave and constant devotion for His benefaction quite like personal God of Semitic religions. As the result of undue emphasis on devotion and worship, Vishishtadvait developed into a vast paraphernalia of elaborate rituals of unproductive idol worship both at home and in temples. This culminated into life-consuming Navadha Bhakti (नवधाभक्ति--9 ways of devotion) and Shodashopachar (षोडशोपचार--16 steps of worship)

Positive contribution of Ramanuj, however, lies in his treatment of all human beings as equal irrespective of their caste and creed and equally eligible for devotion and salvation.

It is Ramanand, 14th in the line of disciples of Ramanuj who brought latter's Vishishtadvait and Bhakti cult to Benaras wherefrom it spread throughout North India. Kabir regarded Ramanuj as his Guru—भक्ती द्राविड़ ऊपजी, लाए रामानंद / कबीर ने परगट करी सात दीप नव खंड।

Madhavacharya (1017-1137 AD) fortified the philosophy of Bhakti by his Dualism (द्वैतवाद), holding Vishnu (also called Hari, Krishna, Vasudeva and Narayan) is not the creator but teacher of Vedas and can be realized with the pramana (प्रमाण) of Vedas. He contradicted Shankar, by holding that all knowledge is intrinsically valid, and the knower and the known are independently real. Both the ritual part (Kramkand) and the knowledge part (Jnanakand) of Vedas are equally valid and interconnected whole. Like Mimasakas, he held that authorless Vedas in all their parts—Samhitas, Brahmanas, Aranyakas and Upanishads-- contain ultimate truth.

In fact, Bhakti cult trying to obliterate caste-distinctions flourished in all the later variants of Vedanta School—Dvaitadvaitvad (द्वैताद्वैतवाद) of Nimbarkachary (12th-13th century) propounding Krishna-centric philosophy of Hansa Sampradaya; Shuddhadvaitvad (शुद्धाद्वैतवाद) of Vallabhacharya (15th-16th century) propounding Pushti Marg centred around Krishna and his Lila as depicted in Bhagavat Puranam; and Achintya Bhedabhedavad (अचिन्य भेदाभेदवाद) of Chaitanya Mahaprabhu centred around Nam-Sankirtan (नाम-संकीर्तन), contending that God is simultaneously one with, and different from, His creation and there is no difference between His holy name and His transcendental form. Bhakti movement later spearheaded by saint and devotee poets in folk languages of different areas received momentum from philosophical discourse of different sub-schools of Vedanta. Ramanujacharya was born in Sriperambadur and established his monastery at Kanchipuram (Tamilanadu), Nimbarkacharya was born and preached in Maharashtra, Madhavacharya was born in Pajaka village near Udupi (Karnataka), then a Pith of Vedanta where he received his education, Vallabhacharya, a Tailang Brahmin of Andhra was born in Varanasi and established his Ashrama at Gokul (Uttar Pradesh), and Chaitanya Mahaparabhu was born at Nabadwip (West Bengal) and preached in Eastern India. Thus, the whole country was stirred by different Bhakti versions of Vedanta philosophy doing away with the caste-distinctions before Bhakti movement began in Hindi heartland and Maharashtra. The common view that Bhakti movement was a by-product of Muslim occupation generating defeatism and loss of faith in the virility and vitality of indigenous religion has no legs to stand. This goes so far as the social impact of later variants of Vedanta School of Vedic philosophy is concerned.

There is also a parallel literary tradition of the emergence of Bhakti cult in Sanskrit before its echo is heard in the literature of folk languages. Shrimad Bhagwat Purana is one of the 18 Puranas and is counted as one of the Mahapurana for its literary excellence particularly of its 10th Canto (स्कंध) and also the popularity of its theme revolving around early life of Krishna besides covering as wide range of subjects as cosmology, astronomy, genealogy, geography, music, dance and yoga. Internal evidence also indicates that it was the first Purana composed by Mythical poet Vyas. Its genesis is discussed in 4rth and 5th chapters of its first Canto. It so happened that, one morning Vyas, after taking bath in holy waters of river Sarasvati, sat down contemplating what he had done and was overpowered by a sense of creative inadequacy. Though, he thought, he had retrieved and edited Veda dividing it in four parts for the good of all the Varnas and Ashramas, had composed Mahabharata for explaining the intent of Vedas for the guidance of women, Shudras and fallen Dvijas who had no right to listen to Vedas, and had religiously followed all his duties (व्रत) and obeyed the elders, his heart was feeling unfulfilled. When he was thus sitting worried and depressed, Devarshi Narada happened to visit him. On being asked the reason of worry by Narada, Vyas candidly told his predicament. Then Narada advised him to compose a text in the praise of Krishna who was up to then neglected by the devotees as something left over although learning, listening and singing of his deeds guaranteed liberation. Vyas follows Narada's advice and the result is composition of Bhagwat Parana in the praise of Krishna as Avatar of Vishnu, for the good of the people in general and women, Shudras and fallen Dvijas having no right to listen to Vedas, in particular. Bhagavat Puran thus became the first literary work devoted to advancement of Bhakti cult. It fulfilled its avowed object so excellently that Vallabhacharya chose this very work for his commentary (सुबोधिनी भाष्य) in support of his philosophy of Suddhadvait and the sect of Pushti Marg that he founded.

The most effective and, in a sense, radical social reform movement in the spirit of Bhakti cult of Vedanta was carried out in Kannad area by Jagjyoti Basaveshwar (Basavanna) in 12th century. Basavanna (1134-1196) was born in a Shaivaite Brahmin family in Bagewadi (North Karnataka). He grew up to become a great scholar, philosopher, poet and social reformer. He spearheaded Shiva-focussed Bhakti movement on the basis qualified philosophy of Vishishtadvait propounded by Ramanuj (supra), treating individual Atman as body of God Shiva, thus identifying Shiva with Atman. Basavanna rejected temple worship with its elaborate rituals under the mediation of Brahmin priests and laid emphasis on devotional worship by treating one's own body as temple. He started a movement against gender and social discrimination, superstition and all kinds of rituals. Instead, he advised his followers called Virshaivas to bear a neckless with the image of Shiva ling to distinguish themselves from orthodox Hindus. He championed the use of vernacular languages in place of Sanskrit. His maternal uncle was Chief Minister of the King of Chalukya (Kalchuri) dynasty and on his death, he was appointed the Chief Minister. His sister Nagamma was married to the Chalukya king. Having considerable influence on the King, he made him deploy considerable funds for aggressing campaigning and implementation of social reforms. In the result, Virshaiva turned into a separate sect from which Lingayat community branched out later. Today, Lingayats and Virshaivas account for major population of certain areas of Karnataka and, being rich, educated and vocal, they control many powerful Mathas and own many educational and medical institutions, wielding considerable influence in State politics.

Thus, major philosophical discourse among the educated class after Shankar revolved around different strands of his monistic philosophy of Vedanta. All these strands advocated Bhakti of some kind or the other as means of knowledge of the ultimate as well as salvation from the bonds of life. At the same time, all strands did their bit to obliterate caste distinction at least in the matter of spirituality and religion and strived to bring egalitarianism in Hindu Dharma and Hindu society. The potent force of Vedanta survived many odds of the medieval period to reappear as Neo-Vedanta in eighteenth century that contributed to the rise of Neo-Hinduism, Hindu Modernism and Hindu Universalism. It is under its benign influence that Raja Ram Mohan Roy (1772-1833) initiated the Brahmo Samaj movement to liberalise Hindu society from the ills of caste system, idol worship and other rituals bordering on superstition and advocating equality of all men, education of women and widow remarriage. Swmi Narayan (1781-1830), a north-Indian Brahmin carried his reform mission to South and assimilated Ashtang Yoga practices in Vedanta philosophy to preach unity, equality and brotherhood, trying hard to improve the lot of poor people, untouchables, Shudras and women and their education. Reforms were carried out by Narayan Guru (1856-1928) too on the same line. He was born in Ezhava caste (presently of OBC status) in Kerala. His vigorous struggle against the oppression of caste hierarchy and for the improvement of the condition of women and their education made him a household name in Kerala as a saviour of humanity. Vivekananda (1863-1902) preached compassion for all beings, tolerance of other religions and basic unity of all religions. He struggled for liberation of the country from the bonds of poverty, illiteracy and superstition. These philosopher-cum-reformers strived to bring in universalism and modernism in the Hindu thought and practices on the basis of Vedantic spirit of Shankar and Ramanuj.

Like earlier Lokayatas, a parallel subaltern tradition of Siddhas (सिद्ध), Nathas (नाथ), Kapalikas (कापालिक), Hathayogis (हठयोगी), Sahajayanis (सहजयानी), Awadhootas (अवधूत), Tantrikas (तांत्रिक) and Vajrayanis (वज्रयानी) was running through the society right from the days of Shankar. All of these were opposed to and even ridiculed Vedas and other Brahmanic texts, Smritis and Puranas, and Varnashram and Caste system, etc. and practiced their own peculiar rituals. Some of the Tantrikas, Hathayogis and Vajrayanis practiced extreme indulgence like Panchmakar (पंचमकार--मांस, मदिरा, मत्स्य, मुद्रा औरमैथुन) and obscure rituals like Shava-Sadhana (शव साधना) and adorned themselves with ash and human skulls or remained naked. The echo of some of these sects is heard in the poetry of Kabir.

Later, Nathas, organized as they were in Guru-Shishya tradition (गुरु-शिष्य परंपरा), became more popular. They had absorbed some of the practices of these subaltern sects and like them, opposed Brahmin texts and Brahmanic social order. Their first Guru is said to be Adinath, that is, Shiva himself. His disciple Matsyendranath was a learned person and spread his sect far and wide. His disciple Gorakhnath (11th-12thcentury) travelled extensively and wrote considerable literature in vernacular. It is Gorakhnath who established a Pith at Gorakhpur (UP) and converted Gurakhas of Nepal into his sect. It is he again who incorporated Yoga-Marg in the form of Hathayoga in Nath sect. Among his disciples were Mayanamati (मयनामती), the mother of King Gopichand of Bengal. Later, Gopichand himself as also another king Bhartihari (भर्तृहरि) or Bharathari became the disciple of Jalandharnath (जालंधरनाथ). Nath tradition continued through Gahininath (गाहिनीनाथ) Nivrittinath (निवृत्तिनाथ) and

Jyananath (ज्ञाननाथ) at least up to 13th century. Their philosophy was an admixture of Sankhya, Yoga and Shaivism which was claimed to be beyond Monism as well as Dualism.

*Navadha Bhakti—श्रवण, कीर्तन, स्मरण, पादसेवन, अर्चना, वंदना, दास्य, सख्य, आत्मनिवेदन।

@Shodashopachar—आवाहन, आसन, पाद्य, अर्घ्य, आचमन, स्नान, वस्त्र, यज्ञोपवीत, चंदन, पुष्प, धूप, दीप (आरती), नैवेद्य, नमस्कार, परिक्रमा, मंत्रपुष्पांजलि।

6

Sant Poets

It is interesting to note that the so-called 'Sant' poets of Nirgun (निर्गुण) category as well as 'Bhakta' poets of Sagun (सगुण) category of Bhakti Cult believed in the supreme reality of incorporeal, pure consciousness (called Brahman in Vedanta philosophy) as the aim of knowledge. But Nirgun poets advocated mystic concept of incorporeal God whereas Sagun poets preferred devotion to a corporeal human Avatar of Brahman as easier way to achieve the aim of life. This dilemma can be well demonstrated by a brief account of the spiritual journey of poet Namadev (1270-1350 AD) of Maharashtra who is normally placed in the category of Sant poets.

Namdev was a contemporary of Sant Jnaneshwr (ज्ञानेश्वर or ज्ञानदेव—1275-1296), a poet, philosopher and Yogi who hailed from a Deshashth Brhmin family and was born in village Apegaon near Paithan. He is regarded as the founder of Varkari school developed around the worship of Vitthal or Vithoba in the temple of Pandharpur. Vithoba is considered to be an Avatar of Vishnu. Although Jnaneshwar belonged to Nath tradition which was opposed to Vedas and Brahmanic social order, his ideas were closer to Advaita Vedanta of Shankar. He, like Gorakhnath, laid emphasis on Yoga but believed in the oneness of Vishnu and Shiva and become an ardent devotee of Lord Vitthal, authoring Jnaneshwari, the first commentary on Gita in Marathi. Namdev, a tailor (शिम्पी in Marathi) by caste, used to sing devotional songs (called Abhanga-- अभंग) in the temple of Vithoba with great passion typical to a Vaishnavite devotee. It is there that he met Jnaneshwar. As tradition goes, Jnaneshwar took him to pilgrimage with other Yogis of Nath sect including his sister Muktabai. All along the journey, Namdev was distraught by the pangs of separation from his lord Vithoba. Jnaneshwar had to explain to him repeatedly that God was not only in the statue but was omnipresent and all-pervasive. He pointed out to Namdev that his devotion was incomplete and, unless he realized the omnipresence of God, he would not achieve the goal of life. At the suggestion of Jnaneshwar's sister Muktabai, a test was carried out. All the saints of the concourse sat down quietly before a potter who started striking on the head of each of them with his stave used for making earthen pitcher. All except Namdev calmly bore the beating (Hathyoga practices had hardened their skull). When Namdev's turn came, he got angry with the potter. Only he out of the group was declared as an unripe pitcher. This was one of the major attempts made by Jnanesgwar to convert Namdev to Yogamarg of Nath sect. Namdev had embraced the stream of Sagun Bhakti without any external help, he was inspired from within by his natural instincts. Jnaneshwar repeatedly emphasized that it was not possible to get real knowledge without the initiation of a Guru.

Jnaneshwar is said to have ended himself by taking Sanjeevan Samadhi at an early age of 21 but Namdev survived to die at a ripe age of 80. To get rid of his dilemma, ultimately Namdev went to a Yogi of Nath sect named Khecharnath and got initiated into that sect. Thereafter, he declared--
सुफल जनम मोको गुरु कीना / दुख बिसार सुख अंतर

कीना. Besides Abhangs in Marathi, after his initiation into Nath sect, Namdev also composed poems in Hindi and addressed to both Hindus and Muslims— हिंदू पूजै देहरा, मुसलमान मसीद / नामा सोई सेविया जह देहरा न मसीद. This is how the two streams of Sagun and Nirgun got merged in Namdev.

The same is more or less true of other saint poets. Kabir became the disciple of Guru Ramanand who initiated him into the tradition of monistic Vedanta through Bhakti cult of Vishishtadvait developed by his Guru Ramanuj. From this Vaishnav tradition, Kabir picked up non-violence and surrender before God. From the Yogis of Nath tradition, he took Nadichakra (नाड़ीचक्र--subtle organism of human body). And from Sufi saints he took the overwhelming power of love. Kabir was thus neither a monist nor a monotheist, nor atheist, nor a Sufi in strict sense of these terms but an admixture of all these plus something more of his own.

In North India, Kabir (1398-1517 AD) and Ravidas or Raidas (1450-1520 AD) were contemporary and pioneers of the tradition of saint poets of Bhakti cult.

Kabir was of course foremost among all Nirgun saints of North India. He was born at Benares in weaver's caste (जुलाहा) which was formerly a middle-ranking caste of Hindus (तंतुवाय) above the untouchables. Strangely enough, all people of this caste had embraced Islam en bloc for some uncertain reasons. But, it seems, this conversion had not improved their social status. It is quite natural that, more than anything else, Kabir was an ardent social reformer. Though he declared Ramanand of Vaishnav tradition as his Guru, he continued to believe in a formless, absolute God. A part of his poetry is also influenced by mystic remnants of Yoga, Awavadhoota, Niranjana, Siddha and Nath traditions. Basically Kabir was an eclectic humanist and was boldly critical of Hindu pantheon of innumerable gods as well as Avatars, and meaningless and farcical rituals practiced in both Hinduism and Islam of his time. While preaching against hypocrisy and bookish knowledge in both the religions and advocating simple, pious and straightforward life, pure and unostentatious love for God, and intuitive wisdom, he continued to earn his livelihood by following his ancestral vocation of weaving clothes. He must have become very popular during his lifetime, drawing people of both Hindu and Muslim religions and diverse castes from far off places. His poems remain as popular and appealing till date as they would have been in his time. A sect in the name of Kabir Panth was formed perhaps after his death and is still alive in India, now there are Kabirpanthi Mathas in a few other countries too. In India, Kabirpanthi Maths are scattered over an extensive area of Uttar Pradesh, Bihar and Chhattisgarh. It is noteworthy that at present, the philosophy and practices of these Maths are not dissimilar from any Vaishnava Math.

Ravidas was born in a Dalit family practicing the vocation of hyde and shoe-making. He was a poet, mystic, social reformer and a spiritual figure venerated as Guru for his austerity and pious life. His influence is still indelible in the areas of Uttar Pradesh, Rajasthan, Gujarat, Maharashtra, Madhya Pradesh and Haryana. He is also regarded to be the founder of Ravidassia sect. He taught removal of social divisions of caste and gender, and promoted unity in the pursuit of personal spiritual freedom. His devotional verses are included in the Sikh scripture Guru Granth Sahib along with those of other saint poets.

Guru Nanak (1469-1539 AD) was born in a Khatri family of Tilwandi village of Lahore district. His father persuaded him to carry on some business by providing him necessary capital which he distributed among the poor and the saints. This incident reflects his saintly, other-regarding character of a recluse from the very beginning. Ultimately, he left his house and family and travelled extensively in search of the right path. It was the time when dogmatic monotheism of Islam was ruling the roost in the area and a large number of people were converted to Islam forcibly and some others had embraced it voluntarily. In the face of this, Nanak was in search of some simple way of worship which could be common to both Hindus and Muslims. He was attracted to Kabir's Nirgun and started preaching the same in Punjab. He used to compose bhajans (devotional songs) and sing them with great devotional fervor. These bhajans (both in Punjabi and Hindi) were later compiled along with the bhajans of other saint poets, in Guru Grantha Sahib (1606 AD). This elevated Nanak to the status of the first Guru of Sikh sect. Unlike Kabir, Nanak didn't revel in complex imagery, allegories and metaphors but preferred to appeal the masses by his simple verses that reflected the humility and straightforwardness of his character.

Dadu Dayal (1544-1603) was another important protagonist of Nirgun School of poetry who founded his 'Dadu Panth.' He was born in Ahmedabad, Gujarat. A legend tells he was found by a Nagar Brahmin as a child floating in Sabarmati River. First, Dadu lived in Aamer (आमेर) for 14 years and then, travelling through Marwar and Bikaner, he reached Naraina village (61 kms from Jaipur) and settled there. In his last days he lived on Bharane hill (13 Kms from Naraina) which grew into the center of Dadupanth. Frequent recurrences of the name of Kabir in Dadu's poetry may be a pointer to the fact that he was Kabir's follower. The meter of his poetry is Doha which resembles Kabir's Sakhis. But the language of his poetry is western Hindi with a mix of Rajasthani as against Khadi and Braj dialects of Hindi of Kabir. He composed some poems in Gujarati, Rajasthani and Punjabi as well. Instead of Kabir's polemics and miraculous expressions, Dadu's poetry expounds the principles of Nirgun with lyrical simplicity. The theme of his poetry encompasses omnipresence and all-pervasiveness of Godhead, imperativeness of Guru, inequity and futility of caste system, basic commonality between Hindus and Muslims, transience of the physical world and the significance of self-realization.

Acharya Ramchandra Shukla has given a short chronological account of five other saint poets of Hindi in North India, namely, Dharmadas (one of the chief disciples of Kabir), Sundaradas, Malukdas and Akkshardas Ananya (अक्षरदास अनन्य).

In Maharashtra, besides Jnaneshwar and Namdeo, other significant poets who flourished after them were Eknath, Tukaram and Ramdas out of whom Ramdas, as a devotee of Ram, clearly belonged to Bhakta category. Vithoba Temple also known as Vitthal-Rukmini Mandir at Pandharpur continued to be the centre of gravity and most of the saint poets sang Abhangas in the praise of lord Vitthal who is regarded an an incarnation of Krishna or Vishnu.

Eknath (1533-1599) is acclaimed as spiritual successor of Jnaneshwar and

Namdev. Like Jnaneshwar, he was born in a Deshashtha Brahmin family of Paithan. He was well-versed in Sanskrit and composed a Marathi variant of Bhagawat Puranam known as Eknath Bhagwat. He also composed a variant of Valmiki Ramayana in the name of Bhavarth Ramayana. Rukmini Swayamvar, Hastamalak, Shukashtak, Swatma-Sukh, Anand Lahari, Chiranjiva-Pad, Gita-Saar and Prahlad-Vijay are his independent works in Marathi. He was a prominent saint of Varkari School. However, his works bear a testimony of his being more of a Bhakta poet of traditional Hindu ethos than a saint poet of Nirgun.

Tukaram (1598/1608—1649/1650) belonged to Kunbi caste (presently in OBC category) and was born in Dehu village near Pune. He is renowned for his contribution to Varkari tradition by composing and singing Abhangas in Marathi in praise of Lord Vithoba also called Pandurang. He also composed devotional songs for community prayers (संकीर्तन). He was influenced by his predecessor saints, Jnaneshwar, Namdev, Eknath and Kabir. Philosophically, he believed in pantheistic Vedantic view of dualism propounded by Ramaanujacharya and Madhawacharya and criticized monism of

Shankaracharya which, according to him, only inflated the ego of learned people declaring themselves as Brahman (अहं ब्रह्मास्मि). He worked for gender equality and accepted ladies also as his disciples and devotees. This was a revolutionary step at the time which invited criticism and even acrimony. When he included a Brahmin lady Bahina Bai as his disciple, her husband created scandal against his wife and also her Guru Tukaram.

It is said, Tukaram didn't die and just disappeared from the scene.

The common factor among all these poets was that they propounded equality of all men and stood against caste hierarchy and untouchability. They can be said to be ahead of their time. But, alas, there is no historical proof of any widespread impact of these saint poets on ostentatious rituals or social behaviour prevalent at the time in masses in general and elite class in particular of Maharashtra or elsewhere.

7

Tradition of Sufi Poetry of Divine Loves

The seeds of Sufism as an ideology are as old as Islam itself. It is said to be the inner dimension of the teachings of Prophet Muhammad (570-632 AD), echoing the spiritual voice of Qur'an. However, these seeds had to wait for germination and for flourishing into a vibrant plant until the golden period of Islamic Caliphate (8th to 10th century). Sufism is said to have come as a counter to material tendencies manifest in the then Islam. Abdullah ibn Muhammad (D. 716 AD) was the first person to be called a 'Sufi.' But a distinct practice of piety associated with introspection could take shape in Baghdad only in the second half of 9th century.

How it reached India? Even prior to the advent of Islam, Arab seafarers were engaged in sea trade along the sea ports of India. Simultaneously, Arab camel caravans carried on trade between India and the West through the land routes of silk and spice up to the Mandi of Constantinople. According to one account, it was a dispute between the Arab sea traders and the local Indian merchants that invited the invasion of Muhammad bin Qasim on Sindh in 711 AD. It is in that year that the Islamic army first entered India and conquered Sindh and Multan connecting India as well as South Asia to the Arab Muslim world. Consequently, mystic tradition which had already reached Persia from Baghdad gained ground in India via Afghanistan, beginning with Kashmir. After this, the trade between India and the Mediterranean Europe carried on by the Muslims flourished peacefully until 900 AD. In 901 a Turk military leader Sabuktigin established his small kingdom in Ghazni (Afghanistan). His son Mahmud Ghaznavi expanded his territories to Punjab by 1027. From there he invaded India several times and plundered many rich Hindu temples besides extending his rule further into India's northwest region. During the early 11th century, the Ghaznavids brought many scholars into northwest India, establishing the first Persian-inspired Muslim culture succeeding prior Arab culture. In 1151, another Central Asian group, called the Ghuris, overtook Ghaznavids and seized their territory. Muhammad Ghuri, a governor of Turkic origin, then initiated a major invasion of India, ultimately extending his territories to Delhi and Ajmer followed by Banaras, Kanauj, Rajasthan, and Bihar, which introduced Muslim rule up to the Bengal region. This facilitated the advent of Sufi intellectualism and many poets and mystics from Central Asia and Iran to settle down in India and get integrated with the indigenous population.

During the rule of Slave dynasty (1206-1290) of Delhi Sultanate, the Mongol invasion penetrated up to Central Asia. The refugees who fled from Central Asia chose India as a safe destination. This historical move proved to be a significant catalyst for the development of Sufi thought in India. Scholars, students, artisans, and common people arrived into the protection of Slave rulers. As the result, the Muslim rule saw immense influx of diverse cultures, religiosity and literature from Persia and Central Asia. Sufism became the main ingredient in all these fields. It spread through various regions and expanded to the Deccan Plateau during the rule of Tughlaq dynasty (1320-1413). Muslim rulers of the Sultanate period were not necessarily orthodox Muslims. Advisors of the dynastic Sultans included Muslim religious scholars (*ulemas*) as well as Muslim mystics (*mashai'kh*). Among the religious elite of this period, two major classifications existed--the *ulemas* and the *faquirs* or Sufi mystics. Ulemas were noted religious scholars who had mastered Islamic legal system of different schools. They were sharia-driven and tended to be more orthodox about Muslim practices. The other group of Faquirs or Sufi mystics was more inclusive and often more tolerant towards non-Muslim traditions. Although the commitment to practice sharia remained a Sufi foundation, early Sufism in India focused on proselytizing through service work and help of the poor. The human and social orientation of Sufism sought to refine the consciousness of the divine, intensify piety, and inculcate a humanistic attitude.

Multiplicity of religious practices and free intellectual discourse among different Hindu sects provided a receptive and fertile ground for spiritual orientation of Sufis. Sufism thus flourished in India not only by conversion of lower caste Hindus but also poetic expression of love and longing for monotheistic God at the exclusion of varied and elaborate rituals prevalent in the Hindu masses. For the Indian poets of Sufi orientation there was a rich crop of folk tales of love that involved suffering and sacrifice which they utilized to transform into divine love, the journey from Ishque Majazi (इश्क़े मजाज़ी) to Ishke haquiqui (इश्क़े हक़ीक़ी).

This is how the tradition of love-torn devotion of Sufi poets was born which ran parallel to the tradition of Nirgun Bhakti of saint poets in Hindi. These Sufi poets not only adopted local Indian language or dialects for their poetry but also chose the subjects for their poetic narrative, the ethos and feelings and the thought process of their characters, their imagery and metaphors from typical Indian milieu.

Kutuban was the first prominent poet of Sufi tradition. He was the disciple of famous Sufi saint Sheikh Burhan of renowned Chishti lineage. Kutuban wrote during early sixteenth century in the court of Husain Shah Shirqi, the Sultan of Jaunpur kingdom. Hussain Shah is famous for his patronage of Islamic learning, oriental knowledge, composite culture, art, architecture and music, he himself being a great musician credited with his contribution to innovation of Khayal style of Indian classical music and invention of many ragas including the popular raga Jaunpuri for the same. Kutuban wrote in this atmosphere congenial to Sufism. He owes his literary fame to his poetic work Mrigavati (मृगावती) completed in 1501-03 AD. Mrigavati is a story of love between the prince of Chandranagar and the princess of Kanchanpur called Mrigavati, depicting the suffering and sacrifice involved on the path of love which Kutuban uses for delineating the intensity of penance in following the devotional path of divine love leading to His realization through self-enlightenment. In between, he aptly describes the principles of Sufi mysticism and its spiritual nuances. Kutuban uses the meters of Doha and Chaupai for narrating his story which style became part of Sufi poetic tradition and was later adopted by Tulsidas for writing his epic work Ramacharitamanas.

Another Sufi poet Manjhan treaded the same path as Kutuban for his poetic narrative of love story picked up from the indigenous milieu and for delineating Sufi philosophy therein. But he excels Kutuban in his literary acumen. Manjhan has praised Sheikh Muhammad Gaus as his pastor and Salimshah Suri (son of Shershah Suri, d. 1545) as the then ruling king according to the practice then prevalent in Sufi poets. Unfortunately, Manjhan's work Madhumalati (मधुमालती) written in the year 1545 is no more available in

full. But even its available fragment
is sufficient to establish the
tenderness of his feelings and
sensitive handling of characters and
events. Just one instance:

बिरह अवधि अवगाह अपारा। कोटि माहिं एक परै त
पारा।।

बिरह कि जगत अँबिरथा जाही। बिरह रूप यह सृष्टि
सबाही।।

नैन बिरह-अंजन जिन सारा। बिरह रूप दरपन संसारा॥

कोटि माँहि बिरला जग कोई। जाहि शरीर बिरह-दुख
होई॥

रतन कि सागर सागरहि, गज मोती गज कोइ।

चँदन की बन बन उपजै, बिरह कि तन तन होइ?

Madhumalti is a story of intense love
between the prince Manohar of the
kingdom of Kanakigiri (कनकगिरि) and
Madhumalti, the princess of the
kingdom of Maharas (महारस). The story
ends happily in their marriage. The
narrative is full of Shringar Ras (श्रृंगार
रस) which the poet regards as the king

of all Rasas--"जो सभ रस महँ राउ रस ताकर करौं बखान". But Shringar Ras in Manjhan blooms on the foundation of love (प्रेम), realization (ज्ञान) and contemplative union (योग). Love accompanied by knowledge and contemplative union with God remained the basic theme of Sufi philosophy. And Manjhan has excelled in enunciation of this philosophy by allegorical story of Madhumalti.

The foremost among the Sufi poets of this genre was undoubtedly Malik Muhammad Jayasi (1477-1542) and his best work was Padmavat which is known as an epic. A disciple of Sufi saint Sheikh Muhiuddin, he was born and lived in Jayas village presently in Amethi district of Uttar Pradesh. He was a contemporary of Shershah Suri and, following the practice of Sufi saint poets, he has profusely praised Shershah's regal eminence in Padmavat--

शेरशाह दिल्ली सुल्तानू। चारहु खंड तपै जस भानू।।

ओही छज राज औ पाट्टू। सब राखे भुइँ धरा ललाट्टू॥

Padmavat was written in the chaste Awadhi dialect with corrupted words of Sanskrit where unavoidable. This dialect is still in vogue in Jayas area. Most probably jayasi's forefathers had embraced Islam a few generations back under the influence of Sufi saints. Hence Jayasi was well-versed in Islamic as well as Hindu traditions besides having very intimate knowledge of the folk life. Most of Padmvat's hand-written copies have been found in Persian script. Thus, Jayasi affected a synthesis between local dialect and foreign script. While laying down the path of pure love in Padmavat, Jayasi has beautifully depicted the life situations of common folk which appeals both Hindus and Muslims alike and forges a common bond between the two.

The first half of Padmavat is purely a poetic imagination but the second half presents an account of characters known to history though controversy subsists on the authenticity of their poetic version. Jyasi's depiction of the character and personality of

Sultan Alauddin, Chittod-King Rana Ratan Singh and the Jauhar of his queen Padmini or Padmavati (पद्मावती), an extraordinary beauty of her time, is borne out from the 'Annals and Antiquities of Rajasthan' (1829) by Col. James Tod who had served as Political Agent of East India Company in the principalities of Western Rajputs.

In the first half of the epic, Padmavati is a young princess of Singhaldweep (सिंहलद्वीप) andher father Gandharvasen (गंधर्वसेन) is worried due to not getting a suitable match for her. She has a parrot named Hiraman (हीरामन) who one day mutters about the King's predicament regarding Padmavati's marriage which he happens to hear. He get angry. Perceiving the king's wrath, Hiraman flew away but was caught by a bird-catcher (बहेलिया) who sold him to a Brahmin of Chittod who, in turn, sold it to the King of Chittod. In course of time the King became very fond of the parrot. One day, when the king was away for hunting, his queen Nagmati (नागमती),

very proud of her beauty, asked the parrot whether there was any other woman in the world equal to her in beauty. The parrot laughed at her and, narrating the beauty of Padmavati, he asserted that there was difference of night and day between the beauty of Nagmati and that of Padmavati. Fearing that the parrot may tell this to the King, Nagmati instructed her maid to kill him. But out of fear of the King, the maid hid him in her home. On return from the hunting, the King, not finding the parrot, became distraught and the maid presented the parrot before him. Hearing of the unmatched beauty of Padmavati from the parrot, the King swooned. Then there is a detailed description of the King being led by the parrot on his long journey to Singhaldweep, and his marriage with Padmavati. On return to Chittod, the King, upset with a trick shown by the royal priest, Raghavchetan (राघवचेतन), orders the priest to leave his kingdom whereupon he goes to Delhi and presents himself before Sultan Alauddin (Khilji). He shows the Sultan a beautiful bangle presented to him by

Padmavati and, describing her matchless, enviable beauty, incites him to attack Chittod. The attack and a long-enduring seize of Chittod fort; peace treaty providing that Alauddin can see Padmavati only in a mirror; his becoming unconscious on seeing her even in this manner; hatching of a conspiracy by him on regaining consciousness, abduction of the King when he comes out of the fort to see Alauddin off and his imprisonment in Delhi. Then Padmavati's tricky message to Sultan to the effect that after having a glimpse of the King she would surrender before him, which he agrees to; march of seven hundred selected soldiers of Chittod led by the two brave Rajput warrior brothers, Gora and Badal from Chittod to Delhi in palanquins under the disguise of Padmavati and her female companions, freeing of the King from bondage in a quick assault on the guards in which Gora is martyred and Badal rescues the King to Chittod, consequent battle of Chittod, martyrdom of the King and self-immolation of Padmavati with other ladies of the royal household in accordance with the old practice of

Jauhar. And on entering the fort Alauddin finds only the ashes of Padmavati mixed with those of other ladies of Chittod's royal household-- all these dramatic developments get a heart-rending touch in the epic. More or less they tally with what is delineated by Col. Tod in his celebrated book on the basis of ballads, traditional tales, legends and historical records kept by the priests in the temples of the area. The challenge to historicity of these developments is indeed notable but, I am afraid, it is not based on any cogent material more authentic than that relied upon by Col. Tod. Such material is in fact unavailable.

What is remarkable here is Jayasi's portrayal of historical characters in the same image and of the related events in the same form as were imprinted in the minds of Hindu populace. Alauddin was always treated as villain and Rana Ratan Singh, Padmavati and the duo of Gora-Badal as heroes of the tragedy by the Hindu population afflicted as they were, from the trauma of victimization during the Muslim rule of Sultanate period, which they regarded as foreign and barbaric. Jayasi was far from the narrow considerations of religion and sects and that has made him a permanent figure in the heart of both Hindus more than of Muslims. He presents a shining example of composite culture and 'idea of India'.

In fact, Padmavat's plot is an allegory of Sufi spiritualism. This has been explained by Jayai himself—

तन चितउर मन राजा कीन्हा। हिय सिंघल, बुद्धि पद्मिनि चीन्हा॥

गुरु सूवा जेहि पंथ देखावा। बिनु गुरु जगत को निर्गुन पावा॥

नागमती यह दुनिया धंधा। बाँचा सोई न एहि चित बंधा॥

राघव दूत सोई सैतानू। माया अलाउदीं सुलतानू॥

[Chittod is the body, King Ratan Singh is the mind (मन), Singhal is the heart and Padmavati is the intellect that identifies the path of liberation. Parrot is the master (गुरु) who leads the King on the way to Singhal, without whom the world is seen as meaningless. Nagmati represents illusory affairs of the world; the one who understands it, becomes free from its bondage. Raghachetan, acting as informer for the Sultan, is Satan and Sultan Alauddin himself is Maya (माया) which creates obstacles in the way of liberation or self-realization, that is the same as God-realization.]

Thus, Jayasi artistically as well as philosophically synthesizes the concept of Satan as found in the mythology of Islam (as also other Semitic religions), on the one hand, and the concept of Maya as found in Vedic philosophy, particularly of Vedanta (वेदांत) or Advaita (अद्वैत) School, on the other. This he does by his own innovation of rendering Satan (or Iblis) created by Qur'anic personal God as an angel, who rebels when asked to bow down before Adam created by Him as the most beautiful creature (Holy Qur'an, 7:11-25) as merely an instrument of all-pervasive Maya. According to Vedanta, Maya is an illusion or bondage created by the temporal world which bond has to be realized as such in order to achieve liberation, that is, self-knowledge, which is the knowledge of the substance, of Brahman permeating all animate and inanimate objects of the universe.

In the depiction of extraordinary beauty of Padmavati, Jayasi realistically borrows the imagery well-known to the folk tradition on the one hand, and renders her beauty as supernatural whose separation ignites spiritual craving of oneness that makes all beings impatient and unquiet, on the other.

Imagery of Folk Tradition:

सरवर तीर पदमिनी आई। खोंपा छोरि केस मुकुलाई॥

ससिमुख, अंग मलयगिरि बासा। नागिनि झाँपि लीन्ह चहुँ पासा॥

ओनई घटा परी जग छाँहा। ससि कै सरन लीन्ह जनु राहा॥

भूलि चकोर दीठि मुख लावा। मेघ घटा महँ चंद देखावा॥

Spiritual Craving of Separation:

बरुनी का बरनौं इमि बनी। साधे बान जानु दुइ अनी॥

उन बानन्ह अस को जो न मारा। बेधि रहा सगरौ संसारा॥

गगन नखत जो जाहि न गने। वै सब बान ओहि के हने॥

धरती बान बेधि सब राखी। साखी ठाढ़ देहिं सब साखी॥

रोवँ रोवँ मानुस तन ठाढ़े। सूतहिं सूत बेध अस गाढ़े॥

Jayasi's Akharavat (**अखरावट**) is a small work containing the elucidation of Sufi concepts and principles, such as, God, creation, living being, love, devotion etc. in the order of alphabets.

Akhiri Kalam (**आख़िरी कलाम**) is a narrative of Qayamat, the end of the creation, which is followed by the Day of Judgement.

The current of love poetry of Sufi tradition in fictional form continued to flow even after Kutuban, Manjhan and Jayasi. During the reign of Jahangir (1605-1627), a Sufi saint poet Usaman (**उसमान**) of Ghazipurwrote

Chitravali (चित्रावली) in 1613 in the same tradition. In the beginning of Chitravali there are verses in the praise of the Prophet, the first four Caliphs and the emperor Jahangir and Usman's pastors (गुरु), Shah Nizamuddin and one Haji Baba. Thereafter, he has given sketchy details of his own life. Thus, he extended the Sufi tradition of praising the pastor and the then ruling monarch by additional inclusions. Chitravali, like Padmavat, is also a narrative of love between Sujan Kumar, the prince of Nepal, and Chitravali, the princess of Rupnagar. In the treatment of its plot, Usman has religiously followed Jayasi. His depiction of the pangs of separation merged with the mood of nature during the six seasons of the country is extremely lucid and rich with typical Indian flavour. From the depiction of Spring (वसंत):

ऋतु बसंत नौतन बन फूला। जहँ तहँ भौंर कुसुम-रंग भूला॥

आहि कहाँ सो, भँवर हमारा। जेहि बिनु बसत बसंत उजारा॥

रात बरन पुनि देखि न जाई। मानहुँ दवा दहूँ दिसि लाई।।

रतिपति-दुरद ऋतुपती बली। कानन-देह आइ कलमली॥

Shaikhnabii (शेखनबी) of Jaunpur and Kasimshah (कासिमशाह) of Barabanki were the later poets of the same genre. Shaikhnabi wrote a love story in the name of Gyandeep (ज्ञानदीप) around 1619, during the reign of Jahangir. Kasimshah wrote 'Hans-Jawahir' (हंस-जवाहिर) around 1721, during the reign of Mughal Emperor Muhammad Shah (Rangila). Gyandeep is a fictional narrative of love between the king Gyandeep and the queen Devajani (देवजानी). And, likewise, Hans-Jawahar is a fictional story of love between the king Hans and the queen Jawahir. Though both have strived to follow the same style and dealt with the similar content, they fall far apart from the literary excellence and philosophical insight of Jayasi's Padmavat.

During the reign of emperor Muhammad Shah (1719-1748) another Sufi poet Noormuhammad (नूरमुहम्मद) flourished in

Jaunpur-Azamgarh area. He wrote Indravati (इंद्रावती) in the Sufi tradition of temporal love assuming spiritual dimensions. It is an imaginary story of love between Rajkunwar (राजकुँवर), the prince of Kalinjar (कालिंजर) and Indravati (इंद्रावती) the princess of Aagamapur (आगमपुर). The text of Indravati begins with the praise of Muhammad Shah in profusion elevating him to the status of a righteous ruler having compassion for all. Noormuhammad has followed the same metric structure as his predecessors—one Doha each after 5 Chaupais. Noormuhammad was a great scholar and most learned among all poets of Sufi love genre. He had written a Diwan in Persian besides another Persian book 'Rauztul Haqaiq' which is unfortunately lost. His Hindi work Anurag-Bansuri (अनुराग-बाँसुरी) written in Persian scriptis spectacular in that it is rich in Sanskrit more than any other Sufi work.

In the beginning of Anurag-Bansuri Noormuhammad had to give a strange clarification:

जानत है वह सिरजनहारा। जो किछु है मन मरम हमारा॥

हिंदू-मग पर पाँव न राखेउँ। का जौ बहुतै हिंदी भाखेउँ॥

This was a time when Hindi, a language enriched by such eminent Muslim poets as Khusao, Rahim and Jayasi in the heyday of Muslim rule was being discarded by the Muslim gentry in search of a new elitist identity in the face of their continuous fall in power, pelf and prestige due to growing influence of East India Company. The readership of Persian literature was continuously shrinking and Urdu was not yet in sight. Noormuhammad must have been criticized for his leaning towards Hindi, particularly Sanskritized Hindi. It must have been viewed as dilution of Muslim identity and inclination towards Hinduism. Hence, the need for his clarification in the beginning of Anurag Bansuri.

Noormuhammad's Indravati proved to be the last work of Sufi love poetry of glorious tradition of Jayasi.

According to Acharya Ramchandra Shukla, by Samvat 1800 (1743 AD) Muslims had started distancing themselves from Hindi. This was the beginning of the preparation of a new ground from which Urdu will spring up one day. But this was to take a time of around 40 years before a new language in the name of Urdu as a language different from Hindi (Hindavi, Dehlvi, Dakni and later Rekhta) will be recognized. This language of literature evolved from the language of conversation prevalent among the Begums and then among the elite Muslims of the Walled City of Delhi, called Urdu-e-Mualla. According to Shamsurrahaman Faruqi, Urdu as a language of literature was unknown until Seventeen hundred Seventies.

8

The Tradition of Sagun Bhakti

Although the genesis of Sagun Bhakti (devotion to corporeal God) is traceable to Ramanujacharya's Vishishtadvaita and Vallabhacharya's Shuddhadvaita variants of Vedanta philosophy, it mainly flourished in North India. Barring Samartha Guru Ramdas of Maharashtra and Narasi Mehta of Gujarat, all other poets of Bhakti cult including Meerabai (Rahasthan) flourished in Hindi belt of North India.

The cult branched out to two distinct currents—Ram Bhakti and Krishna Bhakti. Ramanand, a disciple ofRaghavanand of Kashi (Benares), is regarded to be the progenitor of Rama Bhakti. Ramanand belonged to 14th line of the disciples of Ramanujachary who, besides Vishishtadvaita variant of Vedanta philosophy, had established his 'Shri Vaishnav Sect' (श्रीवैष्णव संप्रदाय) involving worship of Vishnu or Narayan as the favourite (इष्ट) god. Ramanand travelled across the country and converted many people to this Sampraday from different castes including Kabir (of weaver caste), Sen Nai (of barber caste) and Raidas (of Dalit caste). Ramanand brought about a significant change in Shri Vaishnav Sampradaya. Instead of worshipping god Vishnu with his abode in Vaukunth (वैकुंठ), Ramanand adopted Vishnu's avatar Rama as favourite God and Ram Nam as chosen Mantra. In Ramanand tradition Rama is regarded as an ideal of a righteous King showing the path of salvation by devotion to all irrespective of caste and creed. Besides his Sanskrit texts, Vaishnavamatabjabhaaskar (वैष्णवमताब्जभास्कर) and Shriramarchanpaddhati (श्रीरामार्चनपद्धति), he composed several devotional verses in Hindi, some of which find place in Guru Granth Sahib. He established a monastic order known as Vairagi Akhada (वैरागी अखाड़ा) having its seats at Ayodhya, Chitrakut and other places.

The father of Vallabhacharya (1479-1531), a Telugu Barhmin from Andhra, had migrated and settled down in Benares. Vallabhacharya was born in a tumultuous period impending Muslim invasion on Benares and the consequent fear of forcible conversion. His parents, Lakshman Bhatta and Yellamma, were fleeing from Benares when Yellamma, under the strain of frightful journey, gave immature birth to a baby at Champaran (presently in Chhattisgarh) who came to be known as Vallabha. A great scholar of Vedas, Upanishads and Vedanta philosophy, he wrote a commentary on Brahmasutra known as Anubhashya (अणुभाष्य) parallel to those of Shankar and Madhavacharya besides two commentaries on Bhagavat Puranam (सूक्ष्म टीका and सुबोधिनी टीका) regarded as the fountain of Vaishnava Bhakti. He developed what is called Shuddhadvait variant of Vedanta philosophy and established Pushti Marg (पुष्टि मार्ग) centred round divine grace (अनुग्रह or पोषण). It is said; he travelled throughout the country barefoot winning many philosophical debates against the followers of Ramanujacharya and Madhavacharya and ultimately established his seat (गद्दी) in Gokul. His disciple Puranmal Khatri started construction of a grand temple of Shrinathji (Krishna) atop Gowardhan Hill which was completed in 1519. Subsequently, in the reign of Aurangzb, due to his fear in the air, the statue of Shrinath was shifted from this temple by boat to Agra along the river Yamuna and then on bullock cart to Nathadwara near Udaipur where another temple called Haveli was built by Maharaj Raj Singh of Mewar. This title Haveli of the new temple gives name (हवेली संगीत) to a beautiful style of singing devotional songs in chorus (संकीर्तन), that is still alive in that area of Rajasthan and Gujarat.

Vallabhacharya rejected asceticism and monastic life and declared even a householder to be eligible for salvation through loving devotion to God Krishna. In the midst of ongoing Muslim onslaught on Hindu populace his Pushti Marg came as a saviour and spread rapidly to a very large segment of the country, particularly the areas covered by present day Uttar Pradesh, Madhya Pradesh, Orissa, Rajasthan, Gujarat, Tamil Nadu, Karnataka and Andhra Pradesh.

It is difficult to say which of the two streams of Sagun Bhakti—Rama or Krishna--appeared first. Muktibodh, in one of his articles 'मध्ययुगीन भक्ति आंदोलन का एक पहलू' published in Janavikalpa (जनविकल्प), September, 2007, propounds a theory as follows. In North India some orthodox elements of the society got influenced by the movement of Nirgun Saints and entered their fold but they also affected the movement in their own way. Their Puranic mind-set carrying sentimentalism of Krishna-Bhakti started struggling against egalitarian ethos of Nirgun movement. It is this emotive current of Krishna-Bhakti that later gave birth to Tulasi's Ram-Bhakti which, in turn, re-established Varnaashram system that had been marginalized by Nirgun Bhakti movement.

Muktibodh's theory also reflects, though incidentally, the historical order of the two streams of Bhakti. Surdas (1478/93—1563/84), the foremost among Krishna Bhakti poets preceded Tulsidas (1511/1532—1623) in birth but not in death. Their creative lives ran contemporaneously for some time and there is also indication of their meeting at Chitrakut which inspired Tulsi to write Ram Gitavali and Krishna Gitavali. The order presumed by Muktibodh is thus not of such consequence as to support his thesis of Krishnabhakti acting as catalyst for reestablishment of Varnashram system through its next step of Rambahakti.

Suradas appears in Chaurasi Vashnavon ki Varta (चौरासी वैष्णवों की वार्ता) as living at Gaughat (गऊघाट) of Yamuna between Mathura and Agra as a saint poet, composing and singing devotional songs.After the construction of Shrinathji temple on Govardhan Hill, Vallabhacharya once happened to encamp at Gaughat. Surdas visited him and composed and sang a devotional song before him. An impressed Vallabhacharya accepted him as his disciple and asked him to compose lyrical songs on the basis of the stories from Bhagavat Puranam. Later, seeing the sincerity of his devotion and his poetic skill, he entrusted Surdas with the Sankirtan service of Shrinathji temple. Surdas thus embraced Vallabhacharya's Pushti Marg.

When Vallabhacharya took Samadhi at the age of 53, his son and successor Vitthalnath selected eight most significant poets of Pushti Marg and recognized them as Ashtachhap (अष्टछाप) poets. Surdas was foremost among them. Others were Kumbhandas, Permanandadas,

Krishnadas, Chheetaswami, Govindaswami, Chaturbhujdas and Nandadas.

Surdas is credited with the authorship of three works, namely, Sursagar (सूरसागर) being a collection of his independent, lyrical poems or Padas called Gitakavya (गीतकाव्य), Sursaravali (सूरसारावली) and Sahitya-Lahari (साहित्य-लहरी). He has, however, taken the theme of his independent poems (पद) only from tenth Canto of Bhagawat Puranam and stories of the rest are but available in short, sketchy form in a small number of poems. Only sundry segments of the story from the birth of Krishna till his departure to Mathura constitute the theme of Surdasa's independent poems without any thread of storyline. Narrative of story is not Surdasa' cup of tea, he revels in the playfulness of child Krishna, tricky exploits of young Krishna in the midst of love-torn Gopis of Gokul, his Raslila with Gopis and chiefly Radha, multi-faceted and unfathomable love between Radha and Krishna that blooms both in communion and separation into all hues of emotion. Surdas, unlike Tulsidas, is not adept in depiction of varied aspects of social life and folk feelings in totality and philosophical discourse on the tradition of Bhakti and Jnan Marg but he is expert in subtleties, complexities and pervasiveness of love and devotion. His lyricism and the lucidity and softness of Vraj (व्रज) dialect is most suitable for the subjects he dealt with--attraction, love, beauty, playfulness of communion and pathos and pangs of separation. Despite the absence of any structural plot, it is the genuineness of feelings in his lyrical poems of both romantic love with its visual intensity and maternal love with its varied and subtle nuances that endeared Surdas among the sensitive people of not only Vraj but entire Hindi heartland, just as the poetry in Maithili dialect of Vidyapati (1352-1448) on the same theme had done earlier.

Surdas has not entered into polemics to establish the supremacy of Shuddhadvat philosophy of Pushti Marg; that was not his arena. But the poems of his Bhramaragit (भ्रमरगीत) in Surasagar, while keeping lyricism and emotional richness intact, present very powerful and convincing critique of Jnanamarg of Advaita philosophy of which Uddhav (ऊद्धव), the messenger of

Krishna from Mathura, seems to be a protagonist. This is the most impressive and touching part of Surasagar that presents a novel discourse in favour of Vishishtadvait philosophy as against monistic philosophy of Vedanta in a commoner's language and world-view. The articulation and satirical expression of Gopis in favour of the path of love renders Uddhava speechless. It is said, he extended his stay in Gokul and retuned Mathura duly converted to the love path of Gopis.

Three extracts from Bhramaragit:

निरगुन कौन देश कौ बासी।
मधुकर, हँखि समुझाइ, सौंह दै बूझति साँच न हाँसी॥
को है जनक, जननि को कहियत, कौन नारि को दासी।
कैसो बरन, भेस है कैसो, केहि रस में अभिलासी॥
पावैगो पुनि कियो आपुनो जो रे कहैगो गांसी।
सुनत मौन है रह्यौ ठगो-सौ सूर सबै मति नासी॥

+++

उधो, मन नाही दस बीस।
एक हुतो सो गयौ स्याम संग, को अवराधै ईस॥
सिथिल भई सबहीं माधौ बिनु जथा देह बिनु सीस।
स्वासा अटकिरही आसा लगि, जीवहिं कोटि बरीस॥
तुम तौ सखा स्यामसुन्दर के, सकल जोग के ईस।
सूरदास, रसिकन की बतियां पुरवौ मन जगदीस॥

+++

रेख न रूप, बरन जाको नहिं, ताको हमैं बतावत।

अपनी कहौ, दरस ऐसे को तुम कबहूँ हौ पावत?

मुरली अधर धरत है सो, पुनि गोधन बन बन चारत?

नैन विसाल, भौंह बंकट करि देख्यो कबहुँ निहारत?

तन त्रिभंग करि, नटवर वपु धरि, पीतांबर तेहि सोहत?

सूर श्याम ज्यों देत हमैं सुख त्यों तुमको सोउ मोहत?

Acharya Ramchandra Shukla has given a short account of the life and poetry of sixteen other poets (including Ashtachhap poets) of Krishna-Bhakti genre who were either contemporary with, or posterior to, Surdas, namely, Nandadas, Krishnadas, Permanandadas, Kumbhandas, Chaturbhujdas, Chhitswami, Govindaswami, Hitaharivamsh, Gadadhar Bhatta, Meerabai, Haridas (the Music maestro admired as Guru by Tansen, the court musician of Akbar), Madanmohan, Shribhatta, Vyasaji, Rasakhan, and Dhruvadas. Out of them Meerabai (मीराबाई and Rasakhan (रसखान) deserve special mention.

Meerabai (1498-1546) was a sort of revolutionary poetess of Krishnabhakti tradition. Born in Rajput family of Mewar, she was married to King Bhojaraj of Udaipur and shortly became widow. Breaking the tradition of Rajput ladies, she came to love Krishna so desperately as to sing and dance blissfully before his statue. She used to travel between Vrindavan and Dwarka singing devotional songs in temples. She regarded Krishna as her husband and lover and was always engrossed in his thought. In this respect, her devotion falls in the tradition of mystic love as practiced by Alwar lady saint Andal, Chaitanya Mahaprabhu, and Sufi saints who revelled in divine intoxication, trance and mystic union. Meerabai's poems are full of melody and intense longing for Krishna as love incarnate. When she was forbidden by her family from appearing before men in the temples, she declared, there is no man to be shy of, other than Krishna. Her singular devotion to Krishna at the cost of worldly affairs places her in the category of top devotees, earning praise from such saint poets as Nabhadas, Dhruvadas, Vyasji and Malukadas. She was also unique in writing both in Vraj dialect like other Krishna-Bhakta poets as well as

Rajasthani dialect. She is credited with the authorship of four texts—Narasiji Ka Mayara (नरसीजी का मायरा), Commentary on Gita-govind, Rag Govind and Rag Sorath (राग सोरठ). It is not without irony that Meerabai died at Dwarka (and not in Udaipur palace), at a premature age of 48. She is the only woman poet of Krisha-Bhakti genre who is shines like a star of Bhakti movement. Her melodious compositions are copiously used as 'Bandish' in Bhajan style of Indian classical music and are on the lips of common folk.

Rasakhan (रसखान--548-1628) was the title of one Syed Ibrahim Khan, a Pashtun Sardar whose family had migrated from Kabul. According to one account, he was born at a place called Pihani in Hardoi district of Utter Pradesh and was the son of a rich landowner (जागीरदार).He received good education and spoke both Hindi and Persian.He earned singular fame among Muslim poets as devotee of Lord Khrishna whom he regarded as supreme God. He got converted to Vashnavism and, in line with liberal Vaishnav tradition, his devotion to Lord Krishna was both to Sagun and Nirgun forms. But the subject of his poetry was Sagun Lila of Krishna taking different forms such as, Bal-Lila, Ras-Lila, Kunj-Lila, Dan-Lila etc.

According to one source, in his early youth, Rasakhan had fallen in love with a woman who was very proud and behaved arrogantly with him. One day he was reading Persian translation of Bhagavat Puranam and was so moved by unselfish love of Gopis for Krishna that he left his beloved and headed straight towards Vrindavan. There is internal evidence for this episode in his work Prem-Vatika, (a collection of Dohas):

तोरि मानिनी तें हियो फोरि मोहिनी-मान।

प्रेमदेव की छबिहि लखि भए मियाँ रसखान॥

[Withdrawing his heart from the proud woman and breaking her pride, Rasakhan saw the image of the God of Love and became his devotee.]

On coming to Vrindavan, Rasakhan became the disciple of Vitthalnath and that catalysed his poetic talent. Instead of lyrical Padas of Gitkavya in the tradition of Surdas and other poets of Krishna Bhakti cult, Rasakhan chose Kavitta-Savaiya (कवित्त-सवैया) and Doha (दोहा) metres for his devotional poetry. His poetry sprang up from his heart and grew so popular among common people that Rasakhan became another name for Kavitta-Savaiya metre. His poems are in simple Vraj (व्रज) dialect, free from ornamentation and allegories and are so full of lucidity, candour and flow that they became very easy to remember. The simplicity of language and content both make his poetry touch the heart of the people. In this respect, there is no match of his poetry except that of Ghananand (घनानंद). Compilation of his Kavitta Savaiyas is available in his another work 'Sujan Rasakhan'.

Tulsidas is foremost not only among the poets of Ramabhakti genre but all the poets of the tradition of Bhakti movement. He revived the Sanskrit tradition of epic narrative of Valmiki whose Ramayana is traditionally considered to be the first epical composition of Laukik Sanskrit. Tulsidas is synonymous with synthesis between opposites and synergy of the essence of all the strands that he considered valid in his time, so as to compose a whole beneficial and agreeable to all. He was a great scholar, great saint and great poet, and with his eclectic mind-set, he combined together and attempted to revive and restate the Hindu tradition in its entirety in his epic work Ramacharitmanas which remains the most popular text of North India till date. It appeals the heart and mind of both the folk and the elite, surpassing all that existed in his time in its composite content as well as poetic beauty.

Tulsidas strikes a cordial balance between age-old conflict of Shaivism and Vaishnavism. In his all-embracing Rambhakti he combines different elements of Indian demography beset with contradictions and antagonisms in his time as well today. The royals and the commoners; the urban and the rural; the tribals, the forest-dwellers, the aboriginals, and the people of mainstream combine together to forge a grand alliance against the evil. It is Tulsidas who cleared Rama of the blots of Sita-Nirvasan and Shambuk-killing as characterized by Valmiki that could not be removed even by Kalidas (Raghuvansham) and Bhavabhut (Uttararamacharitam). Tulsidas thus converted Rama into Sitaram and found a universal image of this duo—

सिया-राम-मय सब जग जानी। करौं प्रनाम जोरि जुग पानी।।

Tulsidad wrote both in the then language of literature Vraj as well as Awadhi dialect as used by Jayasi but duly refined by literary expressions and Sanskrit words. His experiment of forging Sanskrit words in Awadhi narrative extending its scope and efficacy for learned discourse on philosophy and spiritualism, and his user of all the meters that were ever used in the course of evolution of Hindi besides those prevalent in his time reflect not only his poetic skill but overall holistic mind-set. Thus, he excelled in Chappay metre of hero-centric poetry of Adikal, Pad or lyrical style of Vidyapati and Suradas, Kavitta-Savaiya metre of Bhatta poets and Doha-Chaupai style of Jayasi and other Sufi saints. His poetry is representative of the people of India with all their varied feelings and behaviour such as conjugal love and its beauty both in emotional affection and sensuous affection (श्रृंगार) and familial devotion, classical and folk traditions of knowledge, social values, individual penance and collective rituals and practices and shows the ultimate and universal path of Sagun Bhakti accessible to all irrespective of caste distinctions. He also deplores the ills and evils of the society, its farcical religious practices and degeneration in human values. He laments the neglect of social norms and social welfare by fraudulent practices with lofty claims of different Nirgun and Yogic sects which had degenerated due to influx of illiterate and wily people and taken many absurd forms by his time. Tulsi's Sagun Rambhakti was never divorced from the social norms and social good, Tulsi's Ram being an epitome of righteous behaviour (मर्यादा पुरुषोत्तम) unlike playful Krishna of Suradas. Tuls's socio-political ideal was rule of Ram (रामराज्य) as depicted in Uttarkand of Ramacharitmanas. His range is wide enough to excel in deep insight into subtleties as well as narrative of details combining intensity and extensity. Tulsi is thus unparalleled in his creativity, symmetry of narrative (प्रबंध), sensitivity towards characters and happenings, beauty of combining all elements of true literary expressions and grasp of varied feelings with their subtle nuances.

All said and done, Tulsi was a devotee first and poet later. Intensity of devotion and resultant will power of a genuine devotee creates a parallel world which for him is more real than the actual world full of contradictions, ambiguities, inequities and anomalies. While reading Ramacharitamanas what strikes is Rama is not a thing of past but has a living presence in the mind of Tulsi. He therefore could not see the contradictions and inequities of Varna and caste systems and the discrimination against women, Shudras and Atishudras prevalent during his time and. Despite his cosmopolitan Bhakti, he is unable to feel the pangs of this inhuman system. At times he seems to countenance the privileged position of Brahmins and other caste Hindus. Be that as it may, his Ramacharitamanas remains nearest to the heart of all segments of Hindu society in India as well as in Indian diaspora in Fiji, Mauritius, British Giana, Trinidad and Tobago and such other countries. The popularity of Ramacharatimanas remains phenomenal and unmatched till date.

Acharya Shuka gives a short account of four other poets of Sagun Ramabhakti who followed the footprints of

Tulsidas. They are Swami Agradas, Nabhadas, Pranachand Chauhan and Hridayaram. It is obvious that due to its growing shift on sensuosity Krishnabhakti cult appealed more and more people and survived longer than the Ramabhakti tradition.

Out of the poets of Sagun Bhakti tradition who flourished beyond the contours of Hindi heartland, two gained such prominence as to deserve their place even in the concise account. They are Narasi Mehta (15th century) of Gujarat and Samartha Guru Ramdas (1608-1681) of Maharashtra.

Narasi Mehta was a Bhakta poet of Vaishnava tradition. For the quality and appeal of his poetry and the quantity of his work he is regarded as the first poet (आदि कवि) of Gujarati. He was born in a Nagar Brahmin family at Talaja and later moved to Junagarh. He lost his parents at the age of 5 and lived most of his life in penury. Besides, he had to suffer from being ostracized and scorned by Nagar Brahmins for his association and singing with lower caste devotees. He was also tortured by his elder brother's wife for remaining engrossed in devotion and earning nothing. He had to leave his home and reach

Vrindavan to see eternal Rasaleela of Krishna with Gopis. He composed 22000 verses on conjugal love between Krishna and Radha with the beauty of shringar having allegorical dimensions and intense lyricism. He is well-known for his beautiful devotional poem 'Vashnav jan to tene kahiye je peer parai jane re' (वैष्णव जन तो तेने कहिए जो पीर पराई जाने रे) which was included in Gandhi ji's prayer songs and became popular all over the world.

Sant Ramadas was a saint, poet, philosopher, chronicler and spiritual leader. He was born as Narayan in Jamb village of present day Jalna district of Maharashtra, in a Deshastha Rigvedi Brahmin family, on the occasion of Ram Navami. When he was 7, his father died. He became growingly introvert and was often seen engrossed in divine thought. He fled from his marriage and reached Panchavati (near Nasik) to lead an ascetic life for 12 years in complete devotion to Lord Rama, spending most of his time in meditation, worship and exercise. It is believed, he attained 'enlightenment' at the age of 24 whereupon he adopted the name Ramdas. He then embarked on a pilgrimage and continued travelling across the country for 12 long years. During this extensive journey he witnessed the then prevailing social realities. Besides suffering from natural calamities of flood and famine, atrocities of the Muslim rulers had made the life of people miserable. He later recorded his observations in two of his literary works, namely, Asmani Sultania (आसमानी सुल्तानिया) and Parachakraniroopan (परचक्रनिरूपण) which provide a rare insight into the then prevailing conditions of common people. He also travelled to Himalayas and is believed to have met sixth Sikh Guru Hargobind at Srinagar. During their conversation, Ramdas reportedly asked Guru Hargobind: "I had heard that you occupy the Gaddi (seat) of Guru Nanak who was a tyagi sadhu, a saint who had renounced the world. You possess arms and keep an army and horses. You allow yourself to be addressed as Sacha Patshah, the true king. What sort of a sadhu are you?" Hargobind replied, "Internally a hermit and externally a prince. Arms mean protection to the poor and destruction of the tyrant. Baba Guru Nanak had not renounced the world but had renounced maya- the self and ego." Ramdas is reported to have said, "Yahhamare manbhavati hai" (This appeals to my mind). And that transformed the life of Guru Ramdas.Unlike <u>Warakari</u> saints composing Abhangs in praise of Vitthalswami, Ramdas no more remained a pacifist and his writings included those encouraging militant means to counter the aggressive 'Muslim invaders'.

After his pilgrimage he returned to Mahabaleshwar, a hill station near Satara. It is from there that he arranged and popularised Ramanavami celebrations which were attended by thousands. He is believed to have discovered idols of Rama in the Krishna river.

Ramdas has extensive literature to his credit including <u>Dasbodh</u>, Karunashtakas, Sunderkand, Yuddhakand, Poorvarambh, Antarbhav, Aatmaaram, Chaturthman, Panchman, Manpanchak, Janaswabhawgosavi,Panchsamasi,Saptsam, Sagundhyan,Nirgundhyan,Junatpurush,Sha dripunirup, Panchikaranyog, Manache Shlok and Shreemad Dasbodh.

His language is precise and lucid. His writings are direct and forceful. Apart from <u>Marathi</u>, traces of <u>Sanskrit</u>, <u>Hindi</u>, <u>Urdu</u> and even <u>Arabic</u> can be found in his literature. A

major chunk of his Marathi writings is
in the form of verses.

Ramdas was an exponent of <u>Bhakti Yoga</u>
or the path of devotion. According to
him, total devotion to Rama brings
about spiritual evolution. He
emphasized the importance of physical
strength as well as devotion for full
individual development and admired
warriors for their role in
safeguarding the society. He was of
the opinion that saints must not
withdraw from society. Instead, they
should work for social and moral
transformation. He aimed to
resuscitate the Hindu culture after
its disintegration over several
centuries owing to consistent foreign
occupation. He also called for unity
among the Marathas to preserve and
promote their local culture. Ramdas
frequently expressed his abhorrence
for distinctions based on caste and
creed. He advocated abolition of
social classes and encouraged the
participation of women in religious
affairs.

Ramdas initiated the Samarth sect to
revive spirituality in the society. He
established several *mathas* and
appointed dedicated, selfless,
intelligent and morally incorruptible

members of the sect in charge. He offered women positions of authority in these Mathas. He had 18 lady disciples including Vennabai heading the *matha* at Miraj and Akkabai managing the affairs of mathas at Chaphal and Sajjangad near Satara. He is said to have once reprimanded an aged person who resented women's participation in religious affairs. Ramdas reportedly responded by saying "Everyone came from a woman's womb and those who did not understand the importance of this were unworthy of being called men". According to him, granting women equal status as men is a prerequisite for social development.

Sant Ramdas was thus ahead of his time, he was a sort of revolutionary in real sense of the term and worked lifelong and incessantly for the uplifting the masses, particularly women and downtrodden and the nation as a whole.

Guru Ramadas was a contemporary of Shivaji. An interesting legend goes to connect the two revolutionary personalities. One day Shivaji saw Ramdas begging in the streets. Shivaji sent a chit to him through his companion Balaji to request him to come to his palace (of Raigad?).

Ramdas obliged. Shivaji insisted upon him to take the whole Maratha kingdom and Ramdas agreed. Then Ramdas invited Shivaji to his place next morning.When Shivaji came and requestedRamdas to take him in service for life, Ramdas kept mum. Then both went roaming in the streets with begging bowl in their hands. They returned to a river bank and took the meal prepared by Ramdas. It is then that Ramdas spoke and askedShivaji to rule Maratha kingdom in his name, take the Guru Chaddar (orange flag) for his banner and defend its honor with his life by treating the kingdom as a trust to be ruled justly as if before God. It is after this episode that Ramdas established 11 Hanuman temples at different places in Satara-Kolahapur region to signify physical along with spiritual development. The claim that Ramdas was Shivaji's Guru is seriously contested in history but this legend establishes close connect between Ramdas and Shivaji.

Ramdas also served an inspiration for many 20th-century Indian thinkers and social reformers including Bal Gangadhar Tilak and Ramchandra Dattatraya Ranade.

Current Hindu societal behavior, religious views and understanding of life and existence owes a lot to these saint and Bhakta poets of middle ages. In essence present Hindu mind-set is a making of these poets besides rituals and ceremonies laid down in by Karmakand of Vedas and rationalized in Mimansa school of Vedic philosophy.